CHAKRAS

VINITA RASHINKAR

INDIA • SINGAPORE • MALAYSIA

Notion Press

No. 8, 3rd Cross Street,
CIT Colony, Mylapore,
Chennai, Tamil Nadu – 600 004

First Published by Notion Press 2020
Copyright © Vinita Rashinkar 2020
All Rights Reserved.

ISBN 978-1-64951-635-0

This book has been published with all efforts taken to make the material error-free after the consent of the author. However, the author and the publisher do not assume and hereby disclaim any liability to any party for any loss, damage, or disruption caused by errors or omissions, whether such errors or omissions result from negligence, accident, or any other cause.

While every effort has been made to avoid any mistake or omission, this publication is being sold on the condition and understanding that neither the author nor the publishers or printers would be liable in any manner to any person by reason of any mistake or omission in this publication or for any action taken or omitted to be taken or advice rendered or accepted on the basis of this work. For any defect in printing or binding the publishers will be liable only to replace the defective copy by another copy of this work then available.

"Om Matrye Namah"

For Puja, Amit and Snow

"The day science begins to study non-physical phenomena, it will make more progress in one decade than in all the previous centuries of its existence. To understand the true nature of the Universe, one must think in terms of energy, frequency and vibration."

– Nikola Tesla

CONTENTS

1. Introduction 9
2. The Chakras 13
3. Sankhya 29
4. Yoga 37
5. Karma 49
6. Muladhara Chakra: Stability is Everything 61
7. Swadisthana Chakra: Our Sense of Self 73
8. Manipura Chakra: The Gut-Brain Axis 85
9. Anahata Chakra: Our Inner Temple of Love 97
10. Vishuddha Chakra: Expressing Our Inner Truth 111
11. Ajna Chakra: The Eye of the Soul 125
12. Sahasrara Chakra: Seek and You Will Find 141
13. Conclusion 157

References *165*
Acknowledgements *169*
Also by This Author *171*
The Sri Chakra Yantra Foundation *173*

1
INTRODUCTION

At this very moment, the last sliver of the waning crescent moon is visible in the night sky, but not for long. Soon it will turn into a new moon for a brief time, carrying in its darkness the pangs of a new beginning, an instinct for birthing. It is a seed that will grow with the waxing moon getting larger every night, culminating in a spectacular orb of the most potent Full Moon, bringing a powerful energy of momentum and manifestation. Then it begins to wane slowly again, thus repeating the cycle. The earth and other heavenly bodies spin on their own axis while also moving around the solar system in their own set of rhythms and patterns. Every atom that exists in the Cosmos is forever moving as the electrons spin around in their own orbit, nothing ever resting. We are all infinitely connected to this eternal wheel that is constantly playing out in all of life. As is above, so it is below. We, too, hold within our own beings the wheels of spinning Universal energy, the vortexes of life – the Chakras.

The word "Chakra" in Sanskrit refers to a spinning disk, wheel or a vortex. The concept of Chakras is central to yoga and Ayurveda. Chakras were first described in the Vedas, especially in the *Yoga Upanishads* about four thousand years ago, and one of the most important texts on the subject is the *Shat Chakra Nirupana* by Purnananda Swami. Early Sanskrit texts speak of them both as meditative visualisations combining flowers and mantras and as physical entities in the body. In Tantra, Chakras are envisioned as continually present, highly relevant, a means to psychic and emotional energy; they play an important role in Shaktism along with the concepts of yantras, mandalas and Kundalini yoga in its practice.

The concept of Chakras gained immense popularity in the West when Sir John Woodroffe (also known as Arthur Avalon) translated the *Shat Chakra Nirupana* and the *Padaka Panchaka* into English in the early 20th century in a book titled *The Serpent Power*. This detailed and complex work formed the basis of C.W. Leadbeater's controversial book *The Chakras,* which is largely responsible for the presently held predominant Western view of the Chakras.

My interpretation of the Chakras is closely linked to my interest in Shaktism and Tantra, and I have attempted to assimilate the various versions of the Chakras without excluding the Western perspective. I do not find a reason to disagree with the prevailing Western views because they clearly have their roots in the Shakti Tantra school. I have omitted the mention of deities that reside in each Chakra because I feel they obscure the core study of the subject by bringing in a mythological and religious element. I have also avoided mention of the ruling planet, associated gem stone and other references which I felt were not relevant to the understanding of the concept of Chakras. That apart, I have remained faithful to the ancient Indian Tantra texts while also drawing from Western additions such as ascribing specific states of minds, specific colours and other such elements which I think actually help in understanding the nature of the energy specific to its location in the body.

Virtually all human cultures have some kind of concept of mind, spirit and soul as distinct from the physical body. While it is a common notion to associate the Chakras with the Indian traditions, in reality all cultures and religions have their own interpretations on similar lines of energy systems in the body. References can be found in ancient Egyptian, Chinese and Japanese philosophies while the Kabbala, Celtic and Sufi traditions also contain information about bodily energies. Renee Skuban writes, "The Chakras, when viewed collectively, reflect unified consciousness, or soul. When viewed individually, they reflect different aspects of consciousness, including body, instinct, vital energy, emotions, communication and connection to the Divine."

In order to fully understand the working of the Chakras, it is necessary to first gain some knowledge about the Sankhya philosophy which enumerates the nature of creation and how the five elements came into being. A study of the Sankhya philosophy will explain the nature of the association of the first five Chakras with an element, a sensory organ and an organ of action. Each of the five elements have their own Bija Mantra, which then becomes the sound energy necessary to activate the specific Chakra.

It is also crucial to gain some understanding of what Yoga really means because most people understand Yoga as "Asana", which, while being one of the eight limbs, is merely a preparatory method for the deeper practice of meditation. Yoga is a deep philosophy that outlines a prescription for a way of life that is conducive to good health, well-being and spiritual evolution. Yoga is deeply connected with balancing the flow of prana, directing it inwards to the Chakras and then upward to the Sahasrara.

Since we are told by Vedic seers that the state of our Chakras depends on our vasanas, Karma and samskaras, we will need to understand the theory of Karma as well. We, therefore, begin the book with dedicated chapters on Sankhya, Yoga philosophy and Karma, and then proceed to examine each of the seven Chakras in detail along with their symbolism, physical and mental manifestations, identification of potential blocks and the actions, including a detailed meditation guide that can help bring out a better understanding of the Chakra system.

2
THE CHAKRAS

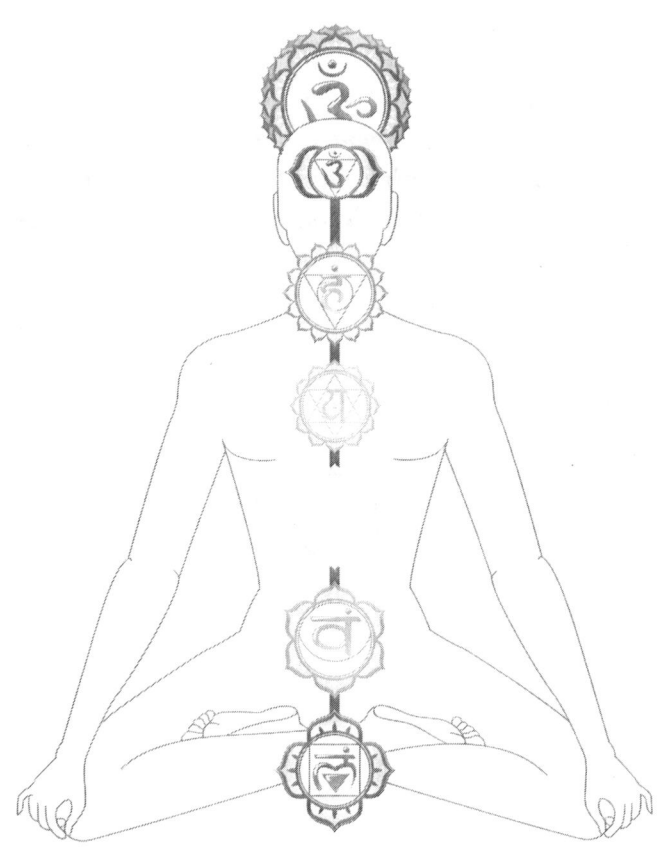

"Yogis know that destiny arises from consciousness defining itself in us through seven major energy centres – the Chakras. The story of the Chakras is the story of how spirit manifests in human form, including our individual variations on the human theme, as well as the story of our spiritual destiny and how we can transform our lives."

– **Sandra Anderson**

There is a single energy that pervades the entire Cosmos. This universal energy – found in everything from the tiniest grain of sand to the mightiest planet – is responsible for the creation and sustenance of life and forms the basis of all existence. Seen at its most fundamental level, matter is merely energy in a state of vibration. We perceive ourselves and the world around us to be made up of physical matter. In fact, it is very difficult for us to conceive that we (and everything around us) are not matter but pure energy. We find it hard to accept this view because we can see, touch and feel objects and so our reasoning mind asks – how can all of this be mere energy?

Matter is made up of atoms at its most fundamental level. Atoms are further made up of protons, neutrons and electrons. Looking deep into the atomic structure shows that everything inside an atom is in the form of waves or vibration. In short, studies in Quantum Physics clearly establish the fact that there is no matter inside of an atom; it is 99.9% empty space and energy is all there is. If the most basic element of creation is made up of only energy, then it stands to reason that everything in the Universe is just that – energy.

How then do we perceive differences in all forms of life? How do we differentiate between a solid object such as a rock, a liquid such as flowing water and gas such as the breeze that we undeniably can feel? The atoms in every form vibrate at a different speed and it is this speed or frequency that determines whether we perceive the energy as solid, liquid or gas. Atoms which vibrate at a slow speed are perceived as dense and tangible (such as the rock), those at a higher frequency are seen as liquid and at the highest speed, we perceive only the intangible such as light or the breeze.

The cells in our body also emit different energies based on where they are located and what functions they perform. These energies are called prana in Ayurveda and "chi" in Chinese medicine. In Ayurveda philosophy, prana is the Sanskrit word for "life-force" or vital principle that permeates all objects – animate and inanimate. Prana flows through several channels, criss-crossing the entire body through energy channels called Nadis. As it flows through the Nadis, prana collects in vortices at particular points in the body which are known as the

Chakras. These key points operate like balls of energy interpenetrating the body.

We can use the analogy of a house to explain the Chakras better. Every house has several electrical connections and wires running throughout the building. Switches located at some key points help operate the electrical equipment and can be turned on or off at will. Similarly, we can see the Chakras as these switches that govern the energy systems in the body. Jayaram V writes, "The main function of the Chakras is to draw in the prana by spinning around their own axes and hold it in their respective sphere to maintain and balance the spiritual, mental, emotional and physical well-being of the mind and body."

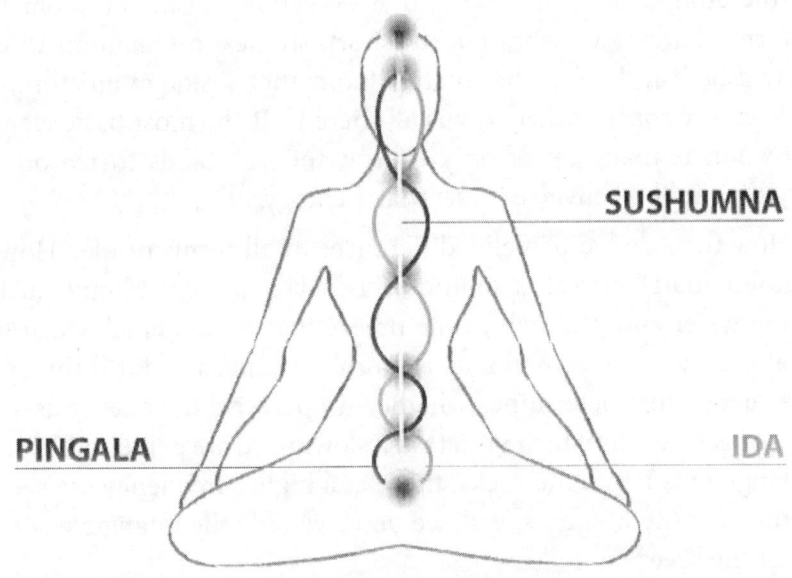

The Tantra texts suggest that the complex network of Nadis are made up of as many as 72,000 channels through which prana circulates in the body. "Nadi" means "stream" in Sanskrit and according to the *Shiva Samhita*, there are fourteen main Nadis that are spread throughout our subtle body. Out of these, the three most important Nadis are:

* Sushumna – the central channel made up of three subtle channels: Vajra, Chitrini and Brahma, through which energy

moves upwards from the Muladhara Chakra to Sahasrara Chakra and controls the central nervous system.

* Ida – the feminine Nadi that is cooling in nature and is associated with the colour white and represents the moon. It journeys from the Muladhara Chakra to the left nostril and controls the parasympathetic nervous system.
* Pingala – masculine in its characteristics, hot by nature and associated with the colour red and represents the sun. It journeys from the Muladhara Chakra to the right nostril and controls the sympathetic nervous system.

Most experts agree that the study of the three main Nadis and seven main Chakras gives a fairly clear idea of the entire energy system in the body. Ancient Indian scholars suggest that there are 114 Chakras (out of which two lie just above the head) in total, but the seven main Chakras lying between the base of the spine and the crown of the head following the curvature of the spine are the most vital. They are:

* Muladhara or Root Chakra
* Swadisthana or Sacral Chakra
* Manipura or Navel Chakra
* Anahata Chakra or the Heart Chakra
* Vishuddha or Throat Chakra
* Ajna Chakra or the Mid-eyebrow Chakra
* Sahasrara Chakra or the Crown Chakra

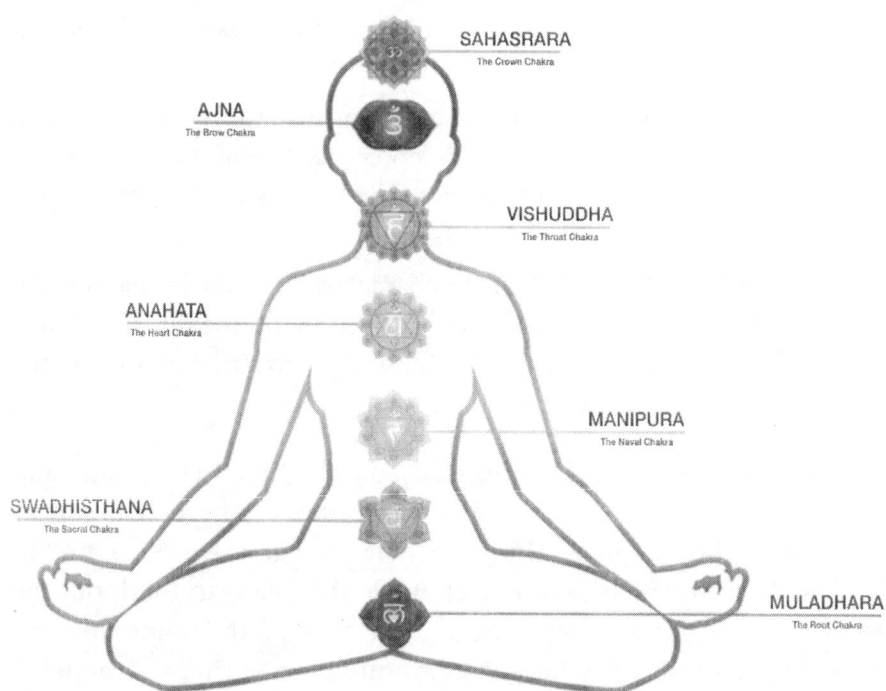

The Nadis and Chakras are not physical attributes. They exist in the subtle body or the Sukshma Sharira. In the Hindu tradition, a living being is made up of mind, body and spirit. The Sharira Tatva (Doctrine of Three Bodies) describes the human body as consisting of three aspects and five sheaths.

The three aspects are:

- Sthula Sharira or the gross physical body
- Sukshma Sharira or the subtle body
- Karana Sharira or the causal body

The Sthula Sharira is the gross physical body through which life or "jiva" is experienced. The main features of this body include birth, ageing and death. It is related to the waking state.

The Sukshma Sharira is the subtle body that houses the mind and vital energies (prana). The subtle body is said to be composed of the five elements (air, fire, water, earth and space) and is made up of the five sense organs (ear, eye, nose, tongue and skin), five organs of action (hand, foot, mouth, anus and genitalia) and the five-fold vital breath (respiration, elimination, circulation, digestion and actions such as sneezing, crying, etc.) along with Manas (mind) and Buddhi (intellect). The dream state is the distinct state of this Sharira. It is in this Sharira that the Chakras can be discerned.

The Karana Sharira is the causal body that merely contains the seed of the Sthula and Sukshma Sharira and it has no other function of its own. It is the most complex of the three bodies and is thought to be the portal to enter higher consciousness. It is identified with the deep sleeping state.

The gross body ceases to exist when death occurs and it then becomes one with Nature. The subtle body disintegrates when it is time to take a new birth, allowing us to develop a new personality in the new life. The causal body incarnates again and again with each rebirth and carries the imprints of the Karmas of our previous lives (samskaras), and disintegrates only at the time of moksha or liberation.

Each body has a dimension or a layer. In Vedanta, this layer is called a sheath or a kosha as it separates the body from the Atman (soul). Each sheath is made up of increasingly finer shades of energy, beginning from the outermost layer of the skin to the innermost spiritual core of our being.

There are five such sheaths and it is in the Pranamaya Kosha that the Chakras operate:

The 5 Koshas

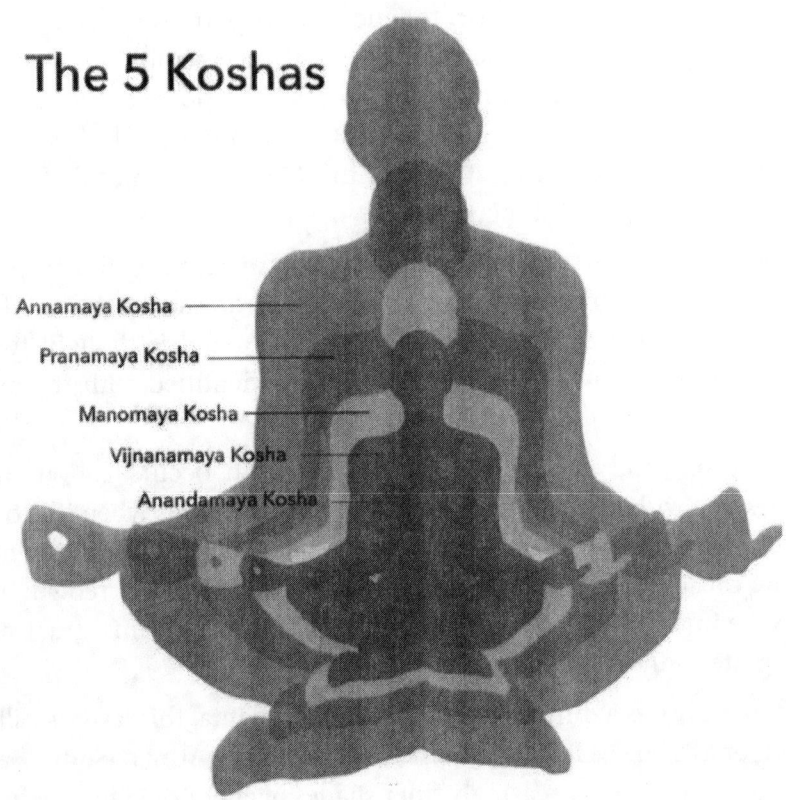

- Annamaya Kosha
- Pranamaya Kosha
- Manomaya Kosha
- Vijnanamaya Kosha
- Anandamaya Kosha

Annamaya Kosha

This is the outermost layer or the physical or food sheath which includes skin, connective tissue, fat, muscle and bone. "Anna" comes from "food" which our bodies take from earth and eventually turn into food. This layer is possibly the one we find ourselves thinking about most of the time to pursue physical gratification and enjoyment.

Pranamaya Kosha

This is the sheath of subtle, vital energy (prana) and includes in it the movement of bodily fluids such as blood circulation, lymph and cerebral fluids and the circulation of breath through the respiratory system. We cannot see energy but can certainly feel it in our bodies. This layer is involved in our intuitions and impulses, and therefore, can be said to control our bodily and spirit rhythm. It is in this kosha that the Chakras operate.

Manomaya Kosha

This is the sheath of the mind and comprises our emotions, feelings and workings of the nervous system. It involves the processing of inputs through our five senses and responding to them reflexively without conscious application of focus. Our thoughts, fantasies and daydreams all constitute this kosha as they are all methods of making sense of the outside world. On the most basic level, we are talking about perceptions, images and emotions, but at a deeper level resides our prejudices, preconceived notions and beliefs that we absorb over a lifetime.

Vijnanamaya Kosha

This is the sheath of wisdom or the psyche. Sensory perceptions coming from the Manomaya Kosha are processed here and meaning is imbued into them with awareness, insight and consciousness. It is here that we make choices about every aspect of living/our lives based on our experiences. This sheath can be seen as the one housing our intelligence as we engage in activities that help us gather wisdom by way of conscious awareness.

Anandamaya Kosha

This is the sheath of bliss as we move from conscious awareness to pure bliss, which includes in it our unconscious mind, samskaras (impressions left behind by every life experience) and our individual consciousness called Chitta. In this sheath, there is nothing but sheer joy and utter contentment. There are no mortal fears or base emotions such as anger, jealousy and insecurities. Among the five sheaths, the Anandamaya Kosha reflects the Divine Consciousness and its state of Satchidananda (eternal bliss).

To understand the development of the process by which energy condenses from the unmanifest to the gross physical form of the human body, we can think of the Anandamaya Kosha as ether or space,

Vijnanamaya Kosha as air, Manomaya Kosha as steam, Pranamaya Kosha as water and Annamaya Kosha as ice. Just as it is more difficult to give shape to ice than to water (as ice is solid and water as a liquid takes on the shape of its container more easily than ice), the various sheaths become more ephemeral as we move towards the higher realms.

Koshas and Associated Limb of Yoga and Chakras

Kosha	Type of layer	Chakra	Related limb of Yoga
Annamaya	Physical	Muladhara	Niyama
			Asana
Pranayama	Energy	Manipura	Pranayama
Manomaya	Mental and Emotional	Swadisthana	Pratyahara
			Dharana
Vijnanamaya	Wisdom	Anahata	Dharana
Anandamaya	Bliss	Vishuddha	Samadhi

All across Vedic literature, it is reiterated that the human body is a microcosm of the Universe. Whatever exists in the Universe is seen in the human body and vice versa. The human body is seen as comprising two portions – the top half beginning at the crown of the head and ending at the tailbone in the spine; the second half beginning at the tailbone and ending at the feet. The spine is the axis on which the body rests just as the Meru is the axis of the Universe. It is for this reason that the spine is called Meru-danda. We find that five of the Chakras lie along this Meru-danda and the final two at the top of the head. The inward journey of a practitioner begins at the base of the spine and moves upward till it reaches a point above the crown of the head.

There are many Chakras located along the hands and feet but these are minor in terms of the role that they play in the overall energy body. Some of the hand Chakras are located in the palms and are seen as an extension of the Anahata or Heart Chakra while some of the foot Chakras are found in the arch of the feet and are governed by the Muladhara or Root Chakra.

The Chakras, even though they are located in the subtle body, have a profound influence on our physical being. Each Chakra's location corresponds to and is associated with organs that lie in its vicinity and with the plexus – a specific group of nerves. Each Chakra is also associated with a major endocrine gland – the gonads correspond to the Muladhara Chakra, the pancreas to the Swadisthana, adrenals to the Manipura, thymus to the Anahata, thyroid and parathyroid to the Vishuddha, the pineal and pituitary to the Ajna and the entire cerebrospinal region to the master Chakra – the Sahasrara.

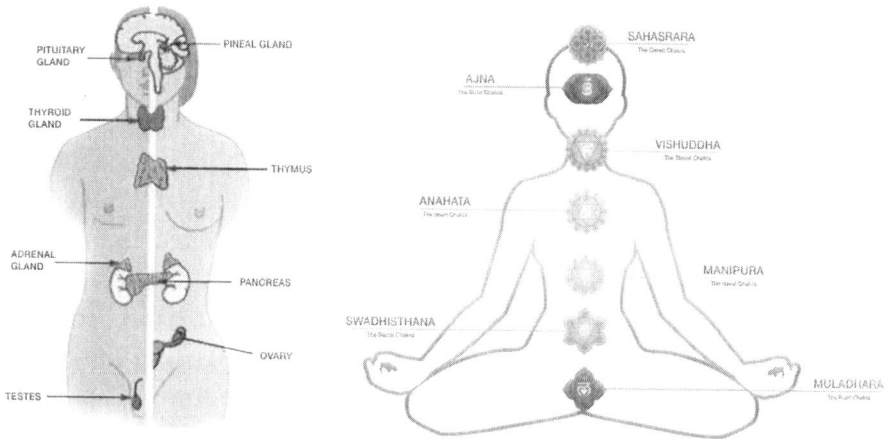

LOCATION OF CHAKRAS AND THEIR CORRESPONDING ENDOCRINE GLANDS

The Chakras not only govern aspects of the physical body but they are also deeply and intrinsically connected to the conscious experience of life itself. All senses, perceptions and states of awareness can be separated in seven categories, which in turn are related to a specific Chakra. When we feel fear, for example, we feel a sensation in the sacral region along with an urge to urinate or defecate. When we feel hurt in relationships, we feel it as a pain or discomfort in the heart region. When we feel unable to communicate, we feel the tightness in our throat Chakra and when we feel stress, it invariably leads to a headache in the Third Eye Chakra. Any discomfort perceived by the sense organs is immediately relayed to the Chakras by way of the nerve plexus connecting the brain to that specific Chakra. Extended discomfort, pain, stress and fear have a way of lodging themselves deeply in the cellular memory of the Chakra, thereby giving rise to blockages, which then lead to illness and disease.

Another significant association of the Chakra system is with the Kundalini Shakti, which has been one of the most popular traditions of spiritual growth in India. Just as in most other traditions, its basic tenet is that Shakti resides within us and spiritual evolution is achieved by proper utilisation of this feminine principle. In the Kundalini tradition, Shakti is seen as residing at the base of the spine at the Muladhara Chakra, symbolised by a serpent coiled into three and a half circles around the central axis Svayambhu-linga at the base of the spine. The three and a half circles represent the three gunas (sattva, rajas and tamas) and the past, present and future while the half turn symbolises the ascent of the Kundalini Shakti to the crown Chakra.

Kundalini comes from the word "serpent" as this energy is shown as lying dormant like a coiled-up snake ready to spring into action. The goal of Kundalini is to open up all the Chakras of the body, thereby allowing the ascent of the energy from the Muladhara to the Sahasrara, traversing through the various Chakras. When the energy finally reaches the top of the head, it is said to bring about enlightenment and liberation of the soul. Vedic texts explain that from the Muladhara Chakra, Ida and Pingala alternate from the right to left sides at each Chakra until they reach Ajna Chakra where they meet again with Sushumna. The rising of the Kundalini is seen as the process of the awakening of spiritual consciousness and brings about liberation from illusion and ignorance, leading to the development of wisdom and ultimately a union with the Universal Consciousness.

"Like flowers, Chakras can be open or closed, dying or budding, depending on the state of consciousness within," says Tiffany Luptak. Why do we need to work on them to ensure that they are open, active and effervescent at all times? All our life experiences, possibly even those from our previous lifetimes, influence our Chakras. We are told by Vedic seers that the state of our Chakras depends on our vasanas, Karma and samskaras. Our negative experiences, feelings and emotions and the low-frequency energy associated with them can bring about a blockage in any one of the energy centres. Blockage of energy leads to a stagnation, which then has a cumulative effect on all the other Chakras. An underactive Chakra may push the adjacent Chakra into excessive energy, thereby causing imbalances across the entire Chakra system.

The reason why we need to bring about a balance of the Chakras is to enable us to clear old blocks and move into higher states of frequency, leading to the evolution of our higher consciousness. This again is in keeping with the philosophy of the Kundalini Shakti.

Like every other aspect of life, the Chakras continuously move from a state of balance to imbalance and vice versa. Disease and ill health are often an outcome of an energy blockage as prana cannot flow freely, thereby affecting the optimal functioning of the body part in question. Imbalances in the Chakras can occur as a result of poor diet, unhealthy lifestyle, lack of exercise, inadequate sleep, bad habits, performance pressure, physical and emotional trauma, stress, unfulfilled and purposeless life, and inability to maintain harmonious relationships with others.

Joy Gardner explains in *Vibrational Healing through the Chakras*, "As we journey through life, we respond to various events by opening up or closing down physically, emotionally, spiritually. Theoretically, a person who is fully enlightened is fully open at all the Chakras and is not susceptible to these kinds of fluctuations."

The Chakras in the Indian tradition correspond to the five elements – Muladhara represents the Earth element, Swadisthana is the Water element, Manipura is the Fire element, Anahata is the Air element and Ajna is the Space element. The progression is from the grossest to the most subtle element, and this ascent can be understood as a spiritual pilgrimage undertaken, starting at the point of the gross self to culminating in the merging of this self with the Universal Consciousness.

In Tantric texts, each of the seven Chakras has a unique symbol represented by a mandala – a spiritual and ritual symbol in Hinduism which represents the Universe. The circular design symbolises the belief that the cycle of life and death is never ending and that everything in the Universe is connected, and even more profoundly that everything is derived from a single source.

The lotus is a common motif that is used to depict the seven Chakras. Each Chakra contains a specific number of lotus petals (starting from four petals in the Muladhara and ending with the glorious thousand-petalled lotus of the Sahasrara), with the unfolding of the petals seen as an expression of the expansion of the soul. Even though a lotus is rooted in muddy waters, the flower itself blooms above the water. The mud said to be symbolic of our own personal attachments and desires and how we are blinded by "maya", while the flower stands as a shining example of beauty, emerging unaffected from an undesirable environment. "Just as the Lotus has its roots in the bottom of the lake, the world is the fertile soil from which we live and grow. But our consciousness is destined to raise itself above the clouded sphere of delusion to the clarity and freedom of Divine vision. The opening lotus blossom symbolises the unfolding of the consciousness and the awakening of wisdom within us. In Yoga literature the Chakras are also referred to as lotuses, for example the Muladhara Chakra is known as the Mula Kamala, the Manipura as Nabhi Kamala, the Vishudda as Kantha Kamala," says Paramahans Swami Maheshwarananda.

In the ancient Indian texts, such as the *Shat Chakra Nirupana*, we do not find associations of the Chakras with colours in the way they are depicted in its present form following the ROYGIB scheme. This association of rainbow colours with the Chakras was first made in the 1970s in a book titled *Nuclear Evolution: Discovery of the Rainbow Body* by Christopher Hills. Chakras are also associated with scents (related to flowers) and gem stones in the Indian texts, but we do not find allusions to the use of crystals for Chakra healing. This is a New Age addition along with other products such as Chakra healing stones, music, bracelets, which present the possibility of commercial gain.

The symbolic representations contained in the mandalas illustrate the qualities of each Chakra, helping us to intuitively discover their attributes by making them relatable and more easily comprehensible to the rational mind. It is important to remember that these symbols are mere representations of the intangible, and therefore, it is always a good idea to use them as a loose guide and stay close to one's perception of the Chakras in recognising and meditating upon them.

Recent studies have been undertaken to understand the Vagus nerve and its connection to the seven Chakras. The Vagus nerve is the 10th cranial ventricle, extending from the base of the spine to the brain. Its function is to gather information from the autonomous organs and glands of the body, such as the heart, intestines, thymus and thyroid, and bring this information to the brain for deduction. The Vagus nerve is the longest nerve in the human body and is often called the communication highway of the body. It does not transmit the chemicals but only the electrical signals to the brain. Yoga and Tantra experts state that there is a distinct possibility that Vagus Nerve could very well be what the sages of old saw "lit up" in deep Samadhi as the fiery serpent running up the spine to the brain. Here are some of the similarities between the Vagus nerve and the Kundalini:

- It runs from the base of the spine to the brain
- The Vagus Nerve is two nerves recognised as one, just as the Kundalini is seen as the intermingling of Ida and Pingala coming together as one in the Sushumna Nadi.
- Both run through the spinal cord.
- Both touch and interact with the organs and glands along the spine.

For those seeking proof that the Chakras exist on a physical level, the similarities between the Kundalini Shakti, as described by Patanjali in the Yoga Sutras, and the Vagus nerve point to the possibility that the Vagus nerve is a physical manifestation of the primordial energy system outlined in the ancient Indian texts.

Swami Tadatmananda describes that whether we believe the Chakras exist or not is actually not a relevant matter to the practice of trying to bring our Chakras to a state of balance. The whole idea behind this wonderful concept is to bring attention and focus to all important parts of our body and meditate upon our feelings that arise there. Just as the goal of a pilgrimage is to get the blessings of a deity residing in a special place, the Chakras must be seen as divinity residing inside our own body which can be visited through a pilgrimage. This inner pilgrimage is a meditation practice in which we deliberately imagine sacred places within our body.

3
SANKHYA

"This declared to you is the Yoga of the wisdom of Sankhya. Hear, now, of the integrated wisdom with which, Partha, you will cast off the bonds of Karma."

– **Bhagavad Gita**

Six distinct, orthodox (Astika) schools of thought and philosophy emerged in ancient India – Nyaya, Vaisheshika, Sankhya, Yoga, Mimamsa and Vedanta. The Sankhya School founded by the learned sage Kapila around 700 BC is one of the oldest and most important among these major ancient Indian philosophic systems and has contributed immensely to the schools of thought that emerged later. This school had a huge influence on the Yoga doctrines, and hence, a study of Sankhya is absolutely required in order to gain a deeper understanding of Yoga philosophy. Sankhya represents the theoretical aspect while Yoga represents the practice of these theoretical aspects. The word "Sankhya" (sometimes also spelt as Samkhya) literally means "number" in Sanskrit. This school of philosophy specifies the exact number of the ultimate constituents of the Universe and enumerates the nature of these constituents, thereby imparting the knowledge of reality. This is the reason why the term "Sankhya" is often figuratively understood to signify "perfect knowledge".

Sankhya is variously seen as a school of atheistic realism and rational dualism. It is atheistic as Kapila asserts that God does not need to exist for the Universe to exist. It is realism as it considers that both matter and spirit are equally real. It is dualistic because it advocates two ultimate realities: Prakriti – nature and Purusha – consciousness.

Sankhya philosophy describes the full spectrum of human existence by revealing the basic elements that make up the macrocosm and the microcosm. It teaches us about the components of the body, mind and spirit, beginning from the gross elements that make up the physical body to the more subtle elements of the mind and consciousness. It names each element, teaches us its function and shows us the relationship each element has with all others.

The individual human being is seen as comprising of 25 distinct, yet related, principles called tattvas or "evolutes" that develop progressively out of one another. The tattvas are guideposts to orient ourselves within the map and to see that what we experience as separate concepts are truly part of a larger whole.

The fundamental principle in Sankhya philosophy is the separation of Brahman (oneness of all elements in the Universe) into two distinct parts: Purusha (pure consciousness) and Prakruti (nature, primeval matter).

Purusha is the first spirit principle of Sankhya; it is neither produced nor can it produce. It is the Knower, the Transcendental Self. It is absolute, imperceptible, immutable, unknowable and can be best described as pure non-attributive consciousness. Prakruthi is the second material principle. It is that which is known, uncaused and eternal. Even though it is not a product, it can produce and has inherent potential to produce. Prakruthi cannot exist without Purusha but Purusha can exist without Prakruthi.

Creation as we know it comes about by a conjunction of Purusha and Prakruthi. Sankhya is not clear about how exactly this conjunction happens but a parallel can be drawn in how a magnet and iron filings are inherently attracted and drawn to one another.

Prakruthi consists of three Gunas or attributes – sattva (balance, luminosity and knowledge), rajas (momentum and desire) and tamas (inertia and decay). When these three qualities stay in equilibrium, then nature stays unmanifested. When this equilibrium gets disturbed by the coming together of Purusha and Prakruthi, nature becomes manifest.

The first evolute of Prakruthi is the Mahat (the Great One) – the cosmic intelligence that evolves out of a preponderance of sattva guna. Prakruthi then gives rise to the "inner senses" which are known as "Antahkarana" or the inner psychic functions:

* Manas – Mind
* Buddhi – Intellect
* Ahamkara – Ego

These enable and guide our psychic and mental processes, and through them we can think, feel, understand and differentiate.

From Mahat arises the Manas or the mind through which we perceive things by receiving impressions from the external world. The mind does not judge or make a choice. It merely records or captures all impressions much like a video camera.

Buddhi is the intellect. It is cosmic intelligence at an individual level, thereby it is the psychological aspect. It processes, co-ordinates and filters the sensory impressions. It decides which of them we accept and pursue further and which ones we reject and drop from further thought.

Ahamkara is the ego which arises out of the cosmic nature of Mahat. It is the sense of self which results in the awareness of "I" and "mine". It literally means "I am the doer". All our feelings, perceptions, ideas and desires are linked to Ahamkara. Ahamkara is the psychic authority that creates the illusion that we are autonomous and different from all other living beings.

Sankhya, then, enumerates the further 20 elements – sense and motor organs which are the "Bahyakaranas" or external organs:

- Jnanendriyas or 5 sense organs (ears, skin, eyes, tongue and nose)
- Karmendriyas or 5 motor organs (tongue, hands, legs, organs of excretion and organs of procreation)
- Tanmatras or the 5 subtle senses (elemental sound, touch, vision, taste and smell)
- Mahabutas or the five building blocks of nature – Space, water, air, fire and earth

The Universe is the result of the combinations and permutations of these 24 tattvas, which together with Purusha (which is an eternal reality) takes the number to 25. Nature makes use of some or all of these tattvas to produce a range of diverse objects and beings which inhabit the world. Of these tattvas, Prakruti is seen as being without a cause. Mahat, Ahamkara and the five tanmatras are both causes and effects. The other tattvas are effects only. Purusha is neither a cause nor an effect. It is eternal, without a cause, and is immutable.

With regard to the tanmatras, Sankhya explains how all the five elements arise out of the previous element. The first physical (gross) element is space which contains within it the other four gross elements of water, air, fire and earth in their subtle form. The subtle quality of space is sound and from the expansion of sound, comes air. The subtle quality of air is touch, and this expands into fire. The subtle quality of fire is vision, and vision expands into water. The subtle quality of water is taste, and taste expands into earth. The subtle quality of earth is smell, and it is said to be the last element to leave the body when death occurs. While one cannot touch, see, taste or smell space, air possesses the qualities of sound and touch (you can feel a breeze and hear its gentle swoosh). Fire can be seen, touched and heard but cannot be tasted or smelled. Water can be seen, touched, heard and tasted but cannot be smelled. Earth, the final manifestation of gross matter, can be seen, touched, heard, tasted and smelled.

Sankhya accepts that there are three valid sources of knowledge:

- Perception
- Inference
- Testimony

This order is important: we use inference only when perception is impossible, and only if both are not present, do we accept testimony as a valid source of knowledge.

Perception is knowledge derived from any of our five senses. In Sankhya, perception is seen as a complex process: when the sense organ comes into contact with an external object, some sensations and impressions reach the mind. These sensations and impressions are perceptual knowledge. The mind then proceeds to process this knowledge and convert it using the other two faculties of buddhi (intellect) and ahamkara (ego). The intellect contributes by bringing about an understanding of this knowledge, while the ego brings its own personal perspective to the knowledge at hand.

In Sankhya, perception is reliable and supplies most of the practical information needed in everyday life, but for this very reason it cannot supply philosophically interesting data. Things that can be seen are not objects of philosophical inquiry. There are many possible reasons why a material object is not (or cannot be) perceived: it may be too far (or near), or it is too minute or subtle; there may be something that obstructs perception. It may be indistinguishable from other surrounding objects or the sensation produced by another object may be so strong as to outweigh it. A fault of the sense organs or an inattentive mind can also cause a failure of perception.

For philosophy, the central source of information is inference, and this is clearly emphasised upon by Isvarakrishna, who recognises three kinds of inference in the Nyaya Sutra:

- cause to effect
- effect to cause
- analogical reasoning

The two constituents of an inference are the sign (the given or premise) and conclusion (inference).

The last valid source of information, i.e., testimony (apta vachana) is the knowledge of objects derived by words. Words could be tradition, text or symbol. "Apta vachana" literally means "reliable speech", but in the context of Sankhya it is understood as referring to the Scriptures.

Sankhya acknowledges that suffering is universal. People find different ways to escape momentarily from the pain – indulging in pleasurable activities such as consuming liquor, eating food which is not healthy, giving in to addictions and so on. On the other hand, others find temporary relief from activities such as the practice of yoga, mindfulness, meditation, charity, etc. Pleasurable activities and mind–body practices only offer a short-term escape. Even the Vedas do not offer a permanent solution as the rewards promised are again temporary at best – after a stay in heaven, one has to face rebirth and go through the rigmarole of more suffering and this cycle continues without end.

Sankhya offers a solution by analysing the fundamental metaphysical structure of the world and the human condition. It finds the ultimate source of suffering – the soul becomes bound when it comes under the influence of Prakruthi and becomes enveloped by delusion and ignorance. When the realisation dawns that Prakruthi is responsible for bondage, the soul strives for liberation and achieves release or freedom from the cycle of births and deaths. According to Sankhya, cutting the root of rebirth is the only way to final emancipation from suffering.

The idea of Prakruti as the sole source of creation and evolution has contributed greatly to the popularity of Tantra and the tradition of Shakti worship. However, its greatest contribution has been towards the formulation of classical yoga, which is modelled on the knowledge derived from the Sankhya school.

Dr Swami Shankardev Saraswati and Jayne Stevenson write: "The personal joy of studying Sankhya is deeply stirring and transformative, as we are learning to unravel the greatest mystery of our lives – ourselves. The Sankhya philosophy systematically deciphers every part of our being, from the lowest level of mortal existence to the highest level of eternal consciousness and spirit. The journey through Sankhya unfolds through three processes: reading (comprehending terminology and philosophy), contemplation and meditation (understanding and feeling the philosophy) and yoga practice (applying the philosophy so that our understanding results in authentic experience)."

4

YOGA

"Yoga is a light, which once lit will never dim. The better your practise, the brighter your flame."

– B.K.S Iyengar

Patanjali drew heavily upon Sankhya philosophy in the development of his *Yoga Sutras,* and many of the practical methods and techniques of yoga rest on Sankhya's philosophical foundations. Yoga takes the Sankhya philosophy into the realm of experience through a gradual and systematic progression. Based on the understanding we gain from Sankhya, we begin the movement towards an understanding of ourselves – starting from the gross or physical level, moving to the subtler levels of mind and spirit, and then returning to the gross with a higher level of consciousness. We return to our "outer" lives rejuvenated and relatively more enlightened.

Sankhya suggests that knowledge is a sufficient means to liberation while Patanjali suggests that systematic techniques/practice (personal experimentation) combined with Sankhya's approach to knowledge is the path to liberation. The *Yoga Sutras* surmise that ignorance is the cause of suffering, and liberation is brought about by the removal of ignorance, which can be achieved through knowledge, discriminative discernment and self-awareness.

Yoga is the oldest system of health and a form of personal development known to mankind. It is a way of life that includes a specific outline of ethics, discipline, prayer and meditation. But in the present time, it has come to be narrowly understood as a form of exercise consisting of physical postures. Yoga means a "union" of the individual self with the absolute consciousness. It is also a union between physical, mental and spiritual energies. This union leads to a healthy and balanced life. Yoga offers its practitioner with a glimpse of bliss that is in fact the true nature of our bodies.

Ancient texts describe yoga as a tree with roots, trunk, several branches, flowers and finally, fruit. They list six different branches, each with its own features and functions, but all of them eventually are paths to personal and spiritual development.

1. Raja Yoga

Raja or "kingly" yoga is a royal approach that focuses on meditation and contemplation. It is based on a strict adherence to the methods outlined in Patanjali's Yoga Sutra and while this branch may appear to recommend an isolated and monastic lifestyle, it can be practised by those who understand that yoga is a path towards self-realisation that can be attained through spiritual devotion.

2. Bhakti Yoga

Bhakti yoga is the path of devotion based on heartfulness and surrender, emphasising that everything in this Universe is divine. It is about acknowledging that divinity lies in every object and every living thing, thereby compelling us to cultivate an attitude of acceptance and love for all. Every thought, word and act offer an opportunity for the practitioner of Bhakti yoga to express love and respect.

3. Jnana Yoga

"Jnana" means "knowledge", and this path of yoga is based on the utilisation of the mind and intellect for spiritual growth. It involves a disciplined study of the scriptures and calls for a constant investigation into the nature of "self". Those who are spiritually inclined with an abiding interest in discovery of self (through introspection and self-study) are more drawn to this path.

4. Karma Yoga

"Karma" means "action" and this path is one of doing. Offering selfless service without any expectations and while remaining detached from the outcome are the main aspects of Karma yoga. In a way, each one of us is a practitioner of Karma yoga as we go about fulfilling our duties and responsibilities in society, but only if we are able to do so without expectation and with a degree of selflessness.

5. Mantra Yoga

This path uses the power of sound and its practice consists of achieving a connection to the Universe and finding centredness through repetitive chanting of mantras. Mantra yoga is a science that engages the mind through focusing on a specific sound for a particular duration through a specified number of repetitions. Repetition of a mantra creates positive vibrations while also helping the practitioner get a glimpse of his own inner divinity. Mantra yoga is often referred to as Japa yoga. "Japa" is a Sanskrit word for the act of repeating mantras.

6. Hatha Yoga

It is the practice of "asana" or yoga postures, using the body as a vehicle for self-transformation involving physical activities. Emma Newlyn writes in *The 6 branches of Yoga* that Hatha yoga is 'The Yoga of Force', "Many teachers equate *Ha* to mean "sun" and *Tha* to mean "moon", and reason that the physical yoga practice is intended to 'balance' the Sun and Moon energies within us. Whilst the physical yoga practice *is* intended to bring about a state of equilibrium within the human organism, the real meaning and essence of Hatha yoga is to change the physical body and mind by way of experimentation, movement and physical 'force'."

The core of Patanjali's Yoga Sutra is an eight-limbed path known as "Ashtanga" (which is not to be confused with a form of yoga popularised by Sri Pattabhi Jois). These eight steps form the structural framework for yoga practice and act as guidelines on how to live a meaningful and purposeful life. The eight steps help in bringing about an awareness of both our mind and body and at the same time, offer strong advice on our moral and ethical conduct, which allows us to lead a life of greater equanimity and peace.

The eight limbs as described in the Yoga Sutras are:

1. Yama – ethical standards and code of conduct
2. Niyama – self-discipline and spiritual practice
3. Asana – body postures
4. Pranayama – breath control
5. Pratyahara – control of the senses
6. Dharana – concentration
7. Dhyana – contemplation
8. Samadhi – oneness with the Universe

The first two limbs serve as a prescription for universal moral and ethical conduct and self-discipline, with advice on how to go about our daily lives – what attitudes we should cultivate, how to manage relationships and how to uphold our personal integrity.

Yama

Yamas deal with our attitude towards external objects and people around us and reinforce the belief that it is our fundamental nature to be compassionate, honest and peace-loving.

There are 5 yamas:

1. Ahimsa or non-violence and compassion towards all
2. Satya or a commitment to truthfulness
3. Asteya or non-stealing
4. Brahmacharya or abstinence and control of senses
5. Aparigraha or non-covetousness

Practising these five guidelines and making them part of our behavioural pattern can not only greatly purify our nature but will also contribute to mental health and happiness of all those around us.

Niyama

Niyamas are rules for personal observances which have to do with inculcating self-discipline and spiritual sadhana or practice. There are five niyamas:

1. Saucha – cleanliness in mind and body
2. Santosha – contentment
3. Tapas – spiritual discipline/ practice
4. Svadhyaya – self-inquiry and study
5. Ishvara pranidhana – surrender to the situation

Niyamas deal with aspects which relate to the inner workings of ourselves and prompt us to look inwards for answers, helping to initiate the desire towards self-enquiry and set us on the path of developing a personal meditation practice. The Niyamas are also related to the koshas (sheaths), leading us from the gross physical body to the most subtle energy that pervades within us.

Asana

Asana refers to a "seat" or position the body assumes during meditation. Yoga prescribes a range of postures which are performed with a particular discipline. They help open up and move energies that have accumulated and stagnated in the energy centres. When stagnant, these energies are responsible for various ailments. When these energies move, they help in healing and restoring a balance to the affected organs. The Yoga Sutras state that a properly executed asana creates a balance between movement and stillness – the state of a healthy body. Asana practice is vital for meditation as it helps to build body discipline and increases the ability to concentrate.

Pranayama

Prana or "life force" is the essence that makes everything in the Universe pulsate with energy. Prana also refers to "breath", and the control of breath by various practices constitutes "pranayama". Breathing or respiration is an unconscious body function which can also become a conscious one if our attention is taken to it. We breathe unconsciously at most times through the day and when we sleep. But we can bring intention to our breath, and Pranayama is the action of consciously controlling our breath for a certain period of time.

Since the eight limbs are concerned with preparing the mind and body for meditation, centring and focusing our breath brings us into a direct awareness of the present moment, thereby preparing us to turn the focus inward.

In addition to this understanding of pranayama as "breath control", there are some experts who also stress on the fact that it needs to be understood as a control of one's prana or vital life-force. In Hinduism,

Prana is said to stem from the "Atman". The soul perceives the experience of the physical world through working of Prana.

Prana is divided into five forms based on its functions:

- Prana vayu (which should not be confused with the master Prana) is the most important of the five energy types flowing in an upward direction and considered to work in the head and chest regions. This prana is responsible for the working of the respiratory system, and also in swallowing and regurgitation of food.
- Apana vayu is a downward-flowing energy considered to work in the pelvic region and is known for its function of elimination from the body which includes faeces, urine and childbirth.
- Samana vayu resides at the navel and is the energy that balances the prana and apana vayu. It is responsible for homeostasis (maintaining body temperature), the process of digestion, assimilation, absorption and working of digestive organs such as stomach, liver and large intestine.
- Udana vayu, which resides at the throat, is the energy that brings about movement by coordinating the neurons of the motor and sensory nervous systems. It governs growth, speech and expression. It also controls the five senses.
- Vyana vayu can be found throughout the body and is the most integrated amongst these five energy types, and flows through the body through the Nadis. In short, it governs circulation on all levels.

Controlling the Prana stimulates the parasympathetic nervous system through the Vagus nerve, which runs from the base of the brain all the way to the abdomen. This nerve is responsible for managing the nervous system responses and regulating heart rate – two of its most important functions. The neurotransmitter acetylcholine is released by the Vagus nerve and plays a pivotal role in increasing calmness and focus.

Regular and long-term practice of pranayama can prevent diseases of the nervous system such as strokes, migraine and Parkinson's. It also works as an anti-ageing factor by reducing stress. It prevents grey cells from diminishing with age, improving memory and focus in the process. An interesting scientific finding about the benefits of pranayama is that the expression of genes involved in stress response can be changed in a way that can potentially slow down the body–mind's reaction to stress.[1]

William J.D. Doran writes in *The Eight Limbs, The Core of Yoga:*

"Pranayama, or breathing technique, is very important in yoga. It goes hand in hand with the asana or pose. In the *Yoga Sutra*, the practices of pranayama and asana are considered to be the highest form of purification and self-discipline for the mind and the body, respectively. The practices produce the actual physical sensation of heat, called tapas, or the inner fire of purification. It is taught that this heat is part of the process of purifying the Nadis, or subtle nerve channels of the body. This allows a more healthful state to be experienced and allows the mind to become calmer. As the yogi follows the proper rhythmic patterns of slow deep breathing, the patterns strengthen the respiratory system, soothe the nervous system and reduce craving. As desires and cravings diminish, the mind is set free and becomes a fit vehicle for concentration.

The first four stages of Patanjali's Ashtanga yoga concentrate on refining our personalities, gaining mastery over the body, and developing an energetic awareness of ourselves, all of which prepares us for the second half of this journey, which deals with the senses, the mind, and attaining a higher state of consciousness."

Pratyahara

Pratyahara is the practice of withdrawing the senses from the stimulation provided by external sources and bring about an enhanced internal awareness. "Ahara" in Sanskrit means "food or nourishment"; hence, pratyahara can be understood as a retreat from the external world to nourish the internal senses. Pratyahara is most easily achieved through a

---

[1] Taken from *Spirituality Decoded* on Instagram

mindfulness in which sensory inputs, such as visuals, sounds, smell and touch, are understood to be external, and hence, allowed to pass without judgement or attachment as one gently draws the mind to return to its inner quietness.

Dharana

Each step of the eight limbs of yoga is meant to prepare us for the next step, and therefore, the practice of withdrawing our attention from the senses sets the stage for dharana or concentration. The objective of dharana is to bring about a steadiness of the mind by focusing its attention upon one particular object (it can be the flame of a candle, a single leaf on a tree branch, the tip of the nose, one's breath, etc.). The object chosen serves no purpose other than to help the mind to stop wandering. Extended periods of concentration can be seen as a precursor to the actual experience of meditation. Dharana, in this sense, can be seen as the first stage in the inner journey towards freedom from suffering. B.K.S. Iyengar states that the objective is to achieve the mental state where the mind, intellect, and ego are "all restrained and all these faculties are offered to the Lord for His use and in His service. Here there is no feeling of 'I' and 'mine'."

Dhyana

"Dhyana" in Sanskrit means a profound, abstract meditation and contemplation or reflection. The root of the word is "Dhi", referring to an imaginative vision which developed into the variant "Dhyana", or meditation.

While Dharana is a state of mind, Dhyana is the process of mind. Dhyana is distinct from Dharana in that the meditator becomes actively engaged with its focus. Patanjali defines Dhyana as the mind process where the mind is fixed on something, and there occurs "a course of uniform modification of knowledge".

Adi Shankaracharya in his commentary on *Yoga Sutras* distinguishes Dhyana from Dharana by explaining Dhyana as the yoga state when there is only the "stream of continuous thought about the object, uninterrupted by other thoughts of different kind for the same object"; Dharana, clarifies Shankara, is focused on one object while remaining aware of its many aspects and ideas. Shankara gives the example of a yogi in a state of Dharana on the morning sun. The Yogi is aware of its brilliance, colour and orbit; the yogi in Dhyana state contemplates on the sun's orbit alone, for example, without his thoughts being interrupted by its colour, brilliance or other related ideas. Thus, we see Dhyana as a state of keen awareness, yet without focus. The awareness is without judgement or attachment and we have all experienced this state at some time in our lives in the "flow state" when we are absolutely absorbed in an activity with such keen awareness that we are oblivious to all external influences.

Dhyana now becomes the step that leads us to a state of Samadhi.

Samadhi

We have now arrived at the final step in the eight-fold path of Yoga. "Samadhi" means "to bring together or to merge". In this state, the senses are at rest (as if in the state of sleep) while the faculties of mind and reason are alert (as in state of wakefulness). It is in this state that one goes beyond consciousness and experiences what it is to be an identity with no distinction from everything else in the Universe. Thus, samadhi refers to union or true Yoga. There is an ending to the separation that is created by the "I" and "mine" of our illusory perceptions of reality. The mind does not distinguish between self and non-self, or between the object contemplated and the process of contemplation. The mind and the intellect have stopped exercising their influence and there is only the experience of consciousness, truth and unutterable joy.

Swami Vivekananda describes Samadhi as: "When one has so intensified the power of dhyana as to be able to reject the external part of perception and remain meditating only on the internal part, the meaning, that state is called Samadhi."

Samadhi is oneness with the object of meditation. There is no distinction between the act of meditation and the object of meditation. Samadhi is a state of ecstatic transcendence, connecting the practitioner with the Divine and showing glimpses of the oneness of everything in the Universe.

The practice of Dharana, Dhyana and Samadhi together is designated as Samyama in the *Yoga Sutras*. Samyama, asserts Patanjali, is a powerful meditative tool which helps us make further progress along the spiritual path. He adds that we must be aware of the three important aspects that support Samyama and they are:

1. Shradda (faith)
2. Virya (indomitable will)
3. Smriti (higher knowledge)

Dr Günther Reisel writes in Yoga in *Daily Life*: "Thousands of years ago, through divine inspiration and meditative visions, the great seers and sages of India developed the science of Yoga. Yoga provides information related to questions concerning our destiny. This knowledge, originally passed down orally, forms the basis of all the great religions of the world. The uniqueness of the Yoga teachings is that they actually provide practical methods of deliverance rather than merely giving theoretical knowledge.

Its basic principles are:

- that we ourselves are responsible for our fate and happiness in life
- that within us lies the ability to free ourselves from the sorrows of life
- that lasting happiness is only found in union with the Divine Self."

As the most highly evolved of all beings, equipped with the capacity to do much more than merely exist and procreate, it is incumbent upon us to become realised human beings, understanding the oneness of everything that exists in creation. Yoga helps us in gaining this understanding and as Paramhans Swami Maheshwarananda says, "Yoga is more than just a system of physical exercises – it is a science of body, mind, consciousness and soul. It is the source of all wisdom and all religions. Yoga makes it possible for every human to discover the real purpose of life and their own true nature. We learn that every injury we inflict on another inevitably comes back to us; that every positive action and every positive thought brings happiness to others as well as to ourselves. Those who have recognised and experienced their own inner truth will never again wage war or use force against others."

5
KARMA

"You are what your deep, driving desire is. As your desire is, so is your will. As your will is, so is your deed (Karma). As your deed (Karma) is, so is your destiny."

– Brihadaranyaka Upanishad

According to Olivia Goldhill, "Consciousness permeates reality. Rather than being just a unique feature of human subjective experience, it is the foundation of the Universe, present in every particle and matter. This panpsychist view is increasingly being taken seriously by credible philosophers, neuroscientists and physicists as traditional attempts to explain consciousness continue to fail." She goes on to explain that "every single particle in existence has an unimaginably simple form of consciousness. This is not to imply that particles have a coherent world view or actively think, merely that there is some inherent subjective experience of consciousness in even the tiniest particle."

Indian philosophy has always held a similar belief that everything in the Universe is interconnected by a common consciousness, and it links all forms of life through the theory of reincarnation or transmigration of the soul. This theory expounds the belief that the soul passes through several lives, taking form as different species, based on its Karma. The Vishnu and Padma Purana state that there are 8.4 million types of living beings which can be categorised as below:

- Nabha Chara – living beings that exist in the air
- Thala Chara – living beings that exist on or under the earth
- Jala Chara – living beings that exist in water

The three types of living beings are further divided into four different classifications in the Garuda Purana based on their method of birth:

- Jarayuja – born of a placenta (viviparous), e.g., humans, cows, elephants
- Andaja – born from eggs, e.g., birds, fish
- Swedaja – born through division, e.g., lower forms of life, bacteria, etc.
- Udbhija – come into being through the sprouting of seeds, e.g., trees, vegetation

Each group possesses its own attributes and aptitudes. While plants and animals not born through Jarayuja have some ability to feel, they are not endowed with the capacity to think or act on their own volition.

Animals born as mammals are more highly evolved with the ability to feel, think, act and discriminate to a limited extent. It is only humans who are endowed with the ability to consciously shape and control our environments with freedom of choice and by exercising a comprehensive discrimination between right and wrong, good and bad, true and false. This sense of self which gives us the ability to make independent decisions comes with a responsibility for our own actions. Hence, the law of Karma applies to humans alone.

"*Tolkappiyam*, the oldest Tamil book dated to 1st century BC, says that living beings are classified in to six categories depending upon the level of their evolution. It placed human beings at the top with 'six senses'. The living organisms with one sense are trees and grass. They have the sense of touch. Living beings with two senses are snails and oysters. They can taste and feel. Beings with three senses of taste, touch and smell are ants and termites. And with four senses are crabs and dragon flies. The fourth sense added here is vision. Living organisms with five senses are horses, elephants, pigs and birds. They have the hearing as the extra sense. Humans are the only living beings with six senses. They have mind, meaning the ability to think." – Santanam Swaminathan, *Knowledge of Biology in Hindu Scriptures*

A human birth, therefore, offers the soul the only opportunity to end the cycle of death and rebirth because of our ability to live more consciously than all other life forms. Only humans are capable of questioning the meaning and purpose of life and only they have the unique ability to find answers to these existential questions. This brings us to the law of Karma.

In our times, the word "Karma" is commonly understood to mean something like retribution or payback, as "in the end, justice will catch up with the wrong doer", which in no way reflects its original meaning. We see posts on social media all the time declaring "Dear Karma, I have a list of people you missed"; "Karma – no need for revenge. Just sit back and wait. Those who hurt you eventually screw up themselves and if you are lucky, you will get to watch." And "Karma is a Bitch".

But what really is the law of Karma, as expounded in the Hindu tradition?

The universal causal law by which good or bad actions determine the future experiences of an individual's existence is known as the law of Karma. This is an autonomous, causal law – no Divine will or external agent intervenes in the relationship of the moral act to its inevitable result. Karma, therefore, represents the ethical dimension of the process of rebirth (samsara). This law suggests that our present lifetime is conditioned by the accumulated effects of actions performed in previous lives, and that future births and life situations experienced therein will be conditioned by actions performed during one's present life. The law of Karma suggests the possibility of a release (moksha) from the cycle of birth and death, while also serving two main functions:

- It provides motivation to live a moral, righteous life
- It offers an explanation as to why evil exists in this Universe

All actions start with a "vasana" or "the seed of one's personality" – subtle remnants from past lives and past actions that remain in the subtle body and take birth again with the gross body. These vasanas are responsible for thoughts which, in turn, produce desires which eventually leads us to act. From where does vasana arise? From our past Karmas. Much like a seed turns into a seedling which grows into a tree and in turn, produces seeds, so also our Karma determines our vasana and in turn, vasana leads to Karma.

The *Bhagavad Gita* lists human actions as belonging to one of these categories:

- Karma – actions which elevate a human's consciousness
- Vikarma – actions which degrade
- Akarma – actions which are neutral, neither good nor bad

We, therefore, create Karma through:

- Our thoughts, intentions, motives
- Our words
- The actions we carry out ourselves
- The actions that are carried out by others based on our inputs

The word "Karma" comes from the Sanskrit verb "kra" meaning "to act". Our Scriptures delineate four types of Karmas:

1. Sanchita Karma

Sanchita or stored Karma is the sum total of all our accumulated Karma from all of our previous lives. Sanchita is the storehouse of every action ever undertaken, and all unresolved actions which await a resolution can be found stored here. It would be impossible to experience and endure all Karmas in one life, and so we bring only a small part of this Karma with us into each birth to resolve and move on.

2. Prarabdha Karma

Prarabdha Karma is that portion of Sanchita Karma that we have chosen to bring into this lifetime. It is therefore action which needs resolution over the course of this lifetime.

3. Kriyamana Karma

Kriyamana Karma is the actionable, present Karma which we are currently actively involved in, and it is also everything that we produce, which then adds up to the Sanchita Karma.

4. Agami Karma

Future actions that result from present actions are known as Agami Karma. In attempting to resolve past Karmas, we inevitably create more Karmas.

Let me try to explain the four Karmas by using a simple analogy. You have a piggy bank in which you put in coins of all kind – tarnished ones and clean, shiny ones. All the coins you have ever put into the piggy bank can be seen as the Sanchita Karma. Now, when you know that there is a forthcoming event for which you will need some money to spend, you remove a certain amount that you deem fit for expenses. This can be seen as the Prarabdha Karma. Some are good coins and some are bad, and based on whether you had more of one kind than the other, there is the likelihood that you will pick more of the one which is abundant. In much the same way, if your Sanchita Karma has more good deeds, then you can expect to be born in better circumstances and lead a more comfortable and fulfilling life. On the other hand, if your Sanchita Karma is filled with bad deeds, then you can expect to face more difficulties and problems. The money that you actually spend out of this withdrawn amount is your Kriyamana Karma. In the process of spending the money, it is possible that you saved some or added a few more coins to what you already had. This goes back into the piggy bank as Sanchita Karma. All the money that you continue to deposit in the piggy bank over the course of the days becomes the Agami Karma or that which will be utilised in the future.

The law of Karma clearly says that each action brings about an energetic vibration which will inevitably return with similar or same qualities at some point in our existence. Our actions, therefore, are the "seeds" of our future and the circumstances of our present birth are nothing but the fruit of our past actions. Does this mean that we accept this "fatalistic" approach and see ourselves as merely puppets in the hands of Karma? Not at all. Even though the events of our destiny are caused and steered as a consequence of earlier actions, in this lifetime as a human, we now have the opportunity to alter the course and reduce the impact through our present actions.

Thus, we are in a position to change the course of our destiny. Through positive actions such as good thoughts, pleasing words, helpful actions, love, forgiveness, gratitude and meditation, we are able to resolve the influence of the Karmas from which we are suffering in this present life, and in this way, we can turn our destiny around for the better. On the other hand, negative thoughts, harsh words, wrongful deeds lead to additional bad Karma, which will then play a role in what we experience in our future lifetimes. Our Vedic texts state that when we die, our physical body perishes but the subtle sheaths persist and they are the repositories of our thoughts, words and deeds. However, since we do not have a physical body when we die, we lose the ability to act, and hence, we await another physical incarnation to resolve our Karmas.

Here, it is also important to understand that we are all influenced not merely by our individual Karma but we also face the repercussions of family Karma, community Karma, national Karma and eventually an Universal Karma, as outlined in the ancient Hindu Scriptures.

It is also important to understand that more than even the action, it is possibly the intention that determines whether the action leads to good or bad Karma. For example, a surgeon goes into the operating theatre with the intention of saving the life of a seriously ill patient who needs urgent surgery. But something goes wrong and the patient dies on the table. Now, will this mean bad Karma for the doctor? No, because his intention was never to cause harm. The patient dies as a result of his own Karma.

In much the same way, negative actions can be of two types. There are those that we perform unconsciously (say for example, a road accident which leads to a death or suffering but not because of any wilful intention on the part of the driver) and those we perform consciously and against our better judgement (a premeditated murder or planned crime). No doubt, the latter action will weigh more heavily because of the wilfulness of the intention. An action whose outcome is bad but which was a result of a mistake or ignorance will not invite as much bad Karma as an intentional act to harm or hurt. The Vedas explain this beautifully stating that poison will do its damage regardless of whether it is consumed unknowingly or taken after knowing its outcome fully well.

One may ask if a negative act can be offset by a positive one. The Vedas state clearly that the law of Karma does not work this way. Each of these deeds will deliver their results independently and it does not help to make a big charitable donation after having committed a crime.

Om Swami further clarifies in *4 types of Karma explained*: At this point, the question may arise – how does one know the difference between a situation which is a result of a past Karma and a situation which is causing us to create a new Karma?

The answer is quite simple. When you do something out of choice; you are creating new Karma, and, when you are forced to do something, you are simply repaying your karmic debt. That's Karma explained. The former will have the consequences – good or bad – drawn up for you; the latter can be tended by managing your karmic store or Sanchita Karma.

In conclusion to the discussion on Karma, I refer to Sadhguru Jaggi Vasudev's note on the subject where he speaks about "How to live with Karma". The primary step, he suggests, is that we have to take responsibility. "Even if what befalls you may be the consequence of collective Karma, but if you want to live an autonomous, full-fledged life – not as a puppet of your heredity or environment – you must first become an individual and stop outsourcing the responsibility to parents, teachers, politicians, countries, god and fate. Karma means becoming squarely responsible for your own destiny." He goes on to add that "Yogic science is about ensuring that the future is no longer a repetition of the past. By refusing to pass the buck, by living consciously, you ensure that you are no longer a victim of collective Karma, but the maker of it. By taking responsibility for your life, you transform not just yourself but also the very planet you inhabit."

Pain, sorrow and suffering are an inevitable part of everyone's journey on this planet. Making an effort to understand their origin and causes while categorising them helps an individual to find his own ways of dealing with and eventually overcoming them. All pain and suffering can be seen as rising from the three miseries which our Vedas called "Tapatreya". They are forces beyond our control which determine the nature of our journeys throughout our life but they are by no means accidental. They adhere to the law of Karma. The three miseries are:

- Adhibhautika pertaining to living beings
- AdhIdaivika pertaining to unseen forces
- Adhyatmika pertaining to the individual (body and mind)

Adhibhautika are the troubles experienced because of other living entities (from external elements, including obstacles imposed by society) like attacks by animals, difficulties in our relationships with people, etc.

AdhIdaivika are experiences which are brought about by higher forces. The word "daiva" can be seen as pertaining to the power of time, nature and the unseen hand. Miseries inflicted upon us by natural disturbances such as earthquakes, droughts, floods, epidemics come under this category.

Adhyatmika are the troubles that we face with suffering of the mind and body. Illnesses such as cancer afflict the body, causing pain and discomfort, while ailments such as depression, schizophrenia and dementia cause mental suffering. Anxiety and stress can also be attributed to this category.

We can only protect ourselves against these through prayer, mantra and Shatsampatti – the six treasures.

1. Kshama – to develop an inner tranquility of the mind
2. Dama – control of the senses and the mind. To restrain oneself from negative actions such as stealing, lying and negative thoughts
3. Uparati – to develop a sense of enthusiasm, to stand above things
4. Titiksha – to be steadfast, disciplined. To endure through and overcome all difficulties
5. Shraddha – intense faith and trust in the Scriptures, in one's guru and most importantly, in oneself
6. Samadhana – to be content in whatever circumstance one finds oneself

"Each one is called a wealth because, like any form of wealth, some of it comes to us easily in life, while others we must make efforts to acquire. Some wealth must be maintained, otherwise it will disappear," says Sri Sri Ravishankar, Art of Living

There are three hindrances to our development on the spiritual path. Offences we may have committed in our previous lives are imprinted upon our samskaras and are carried through into this lifetime. These past actions come up as active hindrances (impurities that need to be cleansed) that inhibit us from spiritual growth and evolution. They cause three types of distortions of the mind:

- Mala – impurity or dirt
- Vikshepa – constant wavering of the mind
- Avarana – a curtain that inhibits us from seeing our real self

Mala is impurity of the mind that is a result of "vasana", as discussed earlier, which needs to be wiped clean before we move further in the journey of evolution to a higher self. Mala is reflected in our desires, lust, anger, attachment and greed. Mala can be removed to some extent by gaining control over our senses and being mindful of our actions.

Vikshepa is mental oscillation or tossing of the mind. It is very difficult to bring about a stillness of the mind and this stillness is an absolute prerequisite for progress on the path of spiritual emancipation. This wayward nature of the mind can be controlled by the practice of meditation, chanting, satsang and eventually, by surrendering oneself to the situation at hand.

Avarana is the curtain of "not knowing" that clouds our consciousness. There is a very interesting story in the Puranas that explains Avarana. A lion cub is left abandoned in a forest upon his mother's death and he has to fend for himself to stay alive. He sees a group of goats grazing nearby. He stays with them as they offer him companionship and solace. Soon, he learns all the habits of the goats and finds no reason to believe that he is any different from them.

One day, after many years, a lion in search of prey, attacks the group and the lion who thinks of himself as a goat. They, along with the lion cub, flee to save their lives. Seeing this, the older lion calls upon the cub and asks him why he is afraid as he is not a goat. The younger lion is surprised as he has no idea that he is anything but a goat. The older lion takes him to the river to show him his reflection in the water. The younger lion then realises his true self.

In the same way, we are all bound to progress on our paths unaware of our mistaken identities about ourselves, and only a realisation of our true nature can free us and put us back on the path in a new light.

Clearly, Karma is a law and not a choice we make. It is a Universal law in the same way that gravity is a law of nature. With every single thought, word or deed we plant a seed and we will have to reap what we sow. The consequence of the seeds that we sow can either be:

- Phala – fruit which is an effect felt in this lifetime
- Samskara – an invisible effect which possesses the ability to transform and determines our experiences in this or future lifetimes

Karma, therefore, is a principle of psychology and once it is truly understood, it offers a great deal of clarity to the meaning and purpose of life. Understanding that we are solely responsible for our present condition is actually a very empowering thought. We no longer feel the need to be victims of either circumstance or chance, and can face life knowing that we are accountable. Therefore, we will choose to lead a more conscious, mindful and intense life. Understanding Karma explains why bad things happen to good people and vice versa and lends to our grasping of the inherent connectedness of everything in the Universe. We understand that suffering and happiness are both related to Karma, and no thought, word or deed is unaccounted for. Hence, good thoughts, words and deeds are the only gateways that can lead us to break the bondage of the life–death cycle and eventually attain moksha or liberation.

6
MULADHARA CHAKRA
STABILITY IS EVERYTHING

"It is in the roots, not the branches, that a tree's greatest strength lies."

Just as roots anchor a plant to the ground and provide the support necessary for it to stand up and withstand the forces of nature, so also the Muladhara Chakra ("mula" means "root" and "aadhara" means "support" in Sanskrit) is the body's most primal and fundamental energy centre, connecting our being with the world and governing our inner sense of security and place in this world.

In addition to providing support, roots also help in nourishing and nurturing the plant. The Muladhara Chakra is the realm that contains our survival instinct and guides our innate abilities to find food, love, balance and safety. Sadhguru says, "The Muladhara Chakra is the foundation of the physical structure and the energy body", which implies that this energy centre is concerned with the physical body.

The Muladhara Chakra represents the earth element whose qualities are heavy, slow, dense and grounding. In the physical body, this Chakra governs aspects of building (strong bones, pliable musculature) as well as eliminating (waste, urine, ejaculation and ovulation) and since it is at base of the spine within the pelvic floor, it is also connected to feet and legs, i.e., the foundation of our bodies which connect us directly to the earth.

In the mental framework, the Muladhara is the centre of primitive and deep-rooted survival instinct and rules over our sex drive, which is the most essential activity to keep the species alive by way of procreation. This Chakra works as a link between our energy body and the physical world, giving us the motivation to eat, sleep and procreate. As regards our psychological make up and spiritual nature, it helps us to develop a sense of belonging and awakens us to the potential of our own higher evolution.

Physically, the Muladhara Chakra is depicted as residing at the perineum in men (between the anus and sex organs in the coccygeal plexus) and at the cervix in women. It is associated with the functioning of the adrenal glands, colon, kidneys, skeleton/bones, muscles and arterial blood that flows through the left chamber of the heart, carrying oxygen and nutrients to our body tissue.

The Muladhara mandala consists of three main symbols:

The Four-Petalled Lotus

The four petals symbolise four aspects of human consciousness: Manas or the mind, Buddhi or the intellect, Chitta or consciousness and Ahamkara or ego. It is here in the Muladhara that our infinite potential of pure conscious existence begins to blossom.

The Square

A square represents stability and rigidity – a stable structure for the other Chakras to rest upon. The four corners of the square can also be seen as representing the four directions.

The Downward-Pointing Triangle

The inverted triangle represents the downward movement of energy and is a reminder of the grounding nature of this Chakra. The tip pointing downwards also indicates that we are at the beginning of our spiritual development; and the sides that spread upwards and outwards show the direction of the developing consciousness.

The animal symbol of the Muladhara Chakra is the seven-trunked elephant – Airavata. An elephant is always associated with strength, stability and support, and in the Hindu tradition, it is revered as giver of prosperity and wisdom. The seven trunks symbolise the Saptadhatus or the seven tissues that make up the physical body. The Saptadhatus are:

- Plasma (Rasa)
- Blood (Rakta)
- Muscle (Mamsa)
- Fat (Meda)
- Bone (Asthi)
- Bone marrow (Majja)
- Semen (Shukra)

Further, the seven trunks can also be seen as representing the seven levels of consciousness:

- Unconscious
- Subconscious
- Dream conscious
- Waking conscious
- Astral conscious
- Supreme conscious
- Cosmic conscious

The fundamental quality of this Chakra is innocence. Innocence is the quality by which we experience pure, child-like joy, without the limitations of prejudice or social and familial conditioning. We see this kind of innocence in small children as their actions are entirely without motive. They love unconditionally and react without affectation to the world around them as they see fit. This innocence is accompanied by an inherent wisdom and instinct that allows them to protect themselves. As a child grows and social interactions increase, this innocence is slowly replaced with a learned behaviour, and this inherent wisdom is lost forever to be replaced by information-based decision making.

The Muladhara Chakra is associated with our sense of smell. Through our sense organ of the nose, we perceive smell – our most primitive human sense. The awakening of the Muladhara Chakra can be experienced by a heightened perception of the senses, seen most acutely in the refinement of the senses of smell and hearing as we become acutely aware of an array of smells and sounds, possibly imperceptible earlier.

The Bija Mantra of the Muladhara Chakra is "Lam". This sound does not have a meaning but it creates a resonance in the related area of the body.

"A mantra is the language of abstract sound much like the language of Mathematics where symbols represent powerful factors, operators and operands that can produce a result and thereby represent or explain any of the phenomena of experience," says N. Krishnaswamy in *The Mantra (For contacting the Divine)*. All sounds emanate from energy and are also manifested as a specific form of energy. Our mental states, emotions and feelings are all affected by specific frequencies and when we expose ourselves in the right manner for a specified length of time to a resonance, it can bring about a balance in the energy centres of the body at both the physical and subtle level.

The colour associated with this Chakra is red, which is often seen as the hue of the earth itself with its dense and heavy nature. Red has the slowest frequency amongst all the colours in the spectrum.

An individual with a balanced Muladhara Chakra exhibits qualities of self-worth, trust and stability. There is a sense of comfort with one's body and a complete acceptance of one's shortcomings, if any. Such a person is good with relationships and is at peace with his family members, colleagues and the world at large.

A balanced Muladhara Chakra is vital because it is the giver of stability, and as Sadhguru says "Stabilizing the foundation is important. Unless the Muladhara is stabilized, one will not know health, well-being and a sense of stability and completeness. These qualities are essential for a human being to make an effort to climb high. You cannot make someone who is shaky on his legs climb a ladder, nor will he be willing. It takes a certain assurance in one's body and mind to walk through life in an efficient and capable manner."

When the Muladhara Chakra is out of balance either because of a deficiency or an excess, it is manifested as discomfort, pain or disease related to the legs (restless leg syndrome, varicose veins,) feet (heel pain, gout), sciatic pain, issues with teeth, hair and nails, problems related to the sexual organs and disturbance in the perception of smell.

In the mind, this imbalance is seen as insecurity, unexplained fears, nightmares, phobias and even Obsessive-Compulsive Disorders. The Muladhara Chakra has to do with our most instinctive and primitive responses, and hence, is responsible for our "fight or flight" modes of response. It is this response that is the primary reason for modern day "stress". Anxiety, panic attacks, depression, suicIdal thoughts and uncontrolled anger can all be an outcome of an imbalance in this Chakra.

At the level of the spirit, a person with an imbalance may only look at life as compromising of the physical, material world with no awareness or desire to learn about the metaphysical or transcendent world. On the other hand, it is also likely that an imbalance could make the person utterly disinterested in the material world and get overly involved and preoccupied with the spiritual realm.

The role of roots in plant kingdom is also to prevent soil erosion, and the Muladhara Chakra also plays the role of holding the social fabric of humanity together by ensuring that we all feel a sense of connection with each other. Just as this Chakra determines our connection with Mother Earth, so also it governs our relationship with our physical mother and any difficulties, problems and issues that arise with her can be resolved as the Chakra gets stronger and clearer.

Sadhguru says in his talks on the Chakras that an entire school of yoga evolved out of the Muladhara – from ways of doing things with the body to reaching one's ultimate nature. "One dimension of yoga that is related to the Muladhara is referred to as Kayakalpa. 'Kaya' means 'body'. 'Kalpa' essentially means 'a long period of time' – we could translate it as eon. Kayakalpa is either about establishing or stabilising the body, or extending its lifespan. There have been many beings who practised Kayakalpa and lived for hundreds of years because they took charge of the most fundamental ingredient in the system, which is the element of earth. It is the earth element that gives us substance. Kayakalpa is about stabilising aspects of the body, which naturally deteriorate with time and in such a way that the deterioration is at least slowed down to a point where it looks like you are ageless and timeless, that you have a kaya that will last for a kalpa, that is, a body that will last for an eon."

The energy flow at each Chakra can either be balanced, deficient or excessive. If the energy flow is balanced, then the body, mind and spirit tend to be in a state of wellness, enjoying a disease-free and painless life, with stress well under control. If the flow is deficient because of a blockage, then there is a sense of discomfort in mind and body, experiencing a sense of sluggishness and a diminished desire for living. If there is too much energy flow to a Chakra, then the mind and body tend to be in a state of agitation, restlessness, and the main emotion may be that of aggression and heightened response to situations. A Chakra experiencing deficiency can be seen as a passive one as opposed to an excessive energy flow seen as an aggressive one. Passive Chakras tend to be protective in nature while aggressive ones tend towards overcompensation.

You can ask yourself the following questions and seek answers by paying close attention to your thoughts, feelings and physical sensations within your body.

- Do I perceive the world as a dangerous place?
- Do I often feel as if I don't belong?
- Do I find myself feeling homesick even when home?
- Do I long to be on the move constantly?
- Do I share a good relationship with my mother and family in general?
- Do I feel a genuine concern for Mother Earth?
- Do I feel connected to Nature or do I feel separated from everything around me?

Here are a few signs that you may be experiencing an imbalance in the Muladhara Chakra:

- You become easily annoyed with people and situations, lash out at others
- You are unable to allow change or to let go of situations, memories
- You tend to obsess about money and possessions
- You have trust issues and are suspicious of other's intentions
- You always feel an urge to escape from the present circumstance
- You have an unhealthy relationship with food (either over eating or anorexia/ bulimia)
- You are too concerned about your physical appearance and constantly worry about your weight and looks
- You feel disconnected from other people and nature
- You experience constant personal, existential and relationship issues

- You are a workaholic
- You feel the need to hoard things which you know you will not have use for in the future

Here are some of the best Muladhara Chakra healing practices:

Find the Courage to Explore the Cause of Your Fears

Take time away from everything to assess the root cause of your fear. Delve into your past to dredge out painful memories, unresolved guilt, deep-seated sorrow and forgive yourself as well as those you feel were responsible. At this time, you can also evaluate your experiences, decisions you have made and let go of regret, if any. Understand that you took a certain decision based on what you knew at that point of time. Make peace with yourself.

Move from a Scarcity Mindset to One of Abundance

The path that your life takes depends to a great extent on the mindset with which you approach life. You can choose to be a person with a scarcity mindset, always living in fear that there will never be enough of anything and that life is one constant hustle to acquire things which you feel are in short supply. Alternatively, you can have an abundance mindset believing that there is always enough of everything for everyone and that the Universe will never leave you lacking for anything, whether its opportunities, money or resource.

Connect with Your Birth Mother

Make peace with your physical mother if your relationship is strained. Forgive any lapses that you perceive in her and seek her forgiveness in return.

Think that you are protected by the Universal Mother and address her in your thoughts, prayers and meditations. Start every day and every endeavour with the mantra "Om Matrye Namah".

Love Your Body

Make peace with your body – instead of constantly being critical of your perceived flaws, find ways to celebrate the features that you like and appreciate yourself more.

Meditate

Meditation not only connects you to a higher spiritual plane, it also helps to ground you. Practice some form of meditation every day, even if it is only for 10 to 15 minutes.

Anchor yourself in an environment that makes you feel safe and secure.

Stay Close to Nature

Connect intimately with Nature – go for walks, have a small kitchen garden, tend to your house plants, smell flowers.

Walking

Walking involves the feet and legs making constant contact with the earth and this helps in healing the Muladhara Chakra.

Kati Basti

An Ayurveda therapy called Kati Basti, which involves application and retention of warm oil on the lower back, is very useful in helping this Chakra heal.

Kegels and Mula Bandha

Women can practice Kegel exercises and both men and women can practice the Mula bandha. It is necessary to learn this practice from a qualified teacher to avoid complications.

Chanting

Chanting or toning sounds can help in balancing the energies of this Chakra. Any mantras associated with Sri Vidya (Lalitha Sahasranama, Trishati, Khadgamala, Sri Suktam) are advisable as they invoke the Universal Mother archetype. You can also practice the chanting of the Bija Mantra "Lam" for 4–5 minutes every day.

Yoga

Some yoga postures which bring the body into contact with the earth can be very helpful in balancing the energies of this Chakra, and they include:

- Mountain pose: Tadasana
- Warrior pose: Virabhidrasana
- Tree pose: Vrikshasana
- Child pose: Balasana
- Lotus pose: Padmasana
- Squatting pose: Malasana
- Easy Pose: Sukhasana
- Corpse Pose: Shavasana

Food

You can add grounding food to your diet and these include groundnuts, root vegetables such as carrots, beetroot and radish. All vegetables with a red hue (tomatoes, strawberry, etc.) also help balance this Chakra.

Aromatherapy

Since this Chakra is closely associated with the sense of smell, aromatherapy is a useful tool for its balancing. Flowery, earthy scents, such as rose, jasmine, oud, patchouli, ylang ylang, sandalwood and rosemary, are the best.

Use Affirmations

Constant self-talk will help reprogram your unconscious mind to be positive and keep out the critical banter that the mind is always involved in. Some of the affirmations you can use are:

- I am grounded and feel secure
- I am worthy of living
- I am connected with my body
- I live in harmony with Mother Earth
- I trust myself and the wisdom of the Universe
- I have all that I need
- I am kind to my body and my mind
- I nourish my mind, body and soul with all the best things
- I am strong, stable and at peace

The Muladhara Chakra carries the imprints of not only our own Karmas but also is a repository of all our ancestral memories and samskaras created within us by unconscious generational patterns. We can free ourselves of our own Karma as well as these patterns by taking responsibility for all of our actions while also strengthening this Chakra. When the Muladhara Chakra is balanced and energy flows freely, you will feel an intense sense of comfort in your own self, a sense of belonging and a sense of having found your place in the world. You will no longer live in insecurity and fear as your thoughts about scarcity of money and belongings recede and you feel a sense of control and start trusting the Universe more. You will find your health improve with better stamina and vitality, and improved thinking and decision-making abilities. You will find that you are more passionate about life and will feel gently connected to others and the world around you. You will slowly realise the futility of the fight and instinctively comprehend that the Universe is actually rigged in your favour, which helps you get superbly aligned with the ebb and flow of life.

7

SWADISTHANA CHAKRA
OUR SENSE OF SELF

"To be yourself in a world that is constantly trying to make you something else is the greatest accomplishment."

– Ralph Waldo Emerson

We now move upwards from the Muladhara Chakra, which is the storehouse of all our past experiences, to the Swadisthana ("swa" meaning "self" and "adhisthana" meaning "primary seat of" in Sanskrit) Chakra where all our past samskaras and vibratory imprints of our previous actions and Karmas are expressed and activated, thus coming to the fore from the unconscious to the subconscious mind. It is in this Chakra that we have the opportunity to control, transform and eventually transcend our base instincts and evolve in our conscious growth and development to a higher realm.

Physically, the Swadisthana is depicted as being located above the pubic bone and below the navel, encompassing the entire pelvic region and the hypogastric plexus. It is associated with the functioning of the spleen, digestive system and reproductive organs (testes and ovaries which produce the hormones testosterone and estrogen respectively that influence sexual behaviours) and all movement of the body.

Mentally, it can be seen as the seat of all our sensations (pleasure and pain), feelings, emotions, and it governs our sense of self-worth and creative impulses. At the spiritual level, it determines our self-image, which in turn governs our relationships and social interactions.

This Chakra has a great deal to do with our creativity. As an outward expression, it governs sexual activity, which eventually leads to the creation of a new life (procreation). In the Muladhara Chakra, sexuality was only considered from the perspective of procreation and propagation of the species. Here in this Chakra, it brings about a desire for union with another being. Inwardly, it is responsible for all our creative impulses, drives and inspirations.

The Swadisthana Chakra represents the water element whose qualities are softness, flexibility and flowing in nature. It is in this water element that all our past imprints are stored in vibratory form. Studies across the globe have confirmed that water does possess the ability to retain memories. Masaru Emoto, a Japanese scientist, has worked for many years to study external influences on water. He elaborates on this concept by exposing water to words, images, music – observing and photographing physical changes to their molecular structure. When water is given positive intention through words such as love, innocence, beauty, etc., it forms beautiful, snowflake-shaped symmetrical crystal structures. When water is exposed to negative words (such as hate, dislike, cancer), feelings and emotions, and even harsh music (such as hard rock), the water forms patterns of asymmetry and disarray.

Even though water can be seen as soft and flexible ("going with the flow"), it can become a force to reckon with when it gathers force, knocking down everything that stands in its way. The energy in the Swadisthana Chakra, once unleashed, must be channelled in a proper fashion in order to ensure that the energy moves upward and onward to the next point of transformation. Many yogis explain the dormant energy of the Kundalini as lying in the Muladhara Chakra in the form of ice (a rigid and solid form of water), waiting for the warmth of our sadhana and spiritual practice to melt the energy into liquid form, allowing it to move along Sushumna Nadi to the Swadisthana Chakra.

As the energy starts to flow in this Chakra, it needs to be steered in the right direction and controlled by our thoughts, words and actions so as to not allow it to dissipate or spiral out of control.

As the energy rises up to the Swadisthana Chakra, it is now forced to come up against our own negative qualities, which are described in Hindu theology as Arishadvarga or Shadripu – the six enemies of the mind:

- Kama – lust
- Krodha – anger
- Lobha – greed
- Mada – pride
- Moha – attachment
- Matsarya – jealousy

Kama means desire in the broad sense of the word and is not limited to the feeling of sexual lust. Desire is natural and required in order for any living being to survive. When our desires are not fulfilled for some reason, then we experience anger, which causes us to become agitated and act in an aggressive fashion. Selfish desires bring about a sense of wanting more and more for oneself, which can also be described as greed. Our desire causes us to think that we are worthy of having certain things (whether it is a material possession or love) and this gives rise to pride. We feel we are better than others and so we start displaying entitled behaviour. Whether our desire is fulfilled or not, we start obsessing about the object, which gives rise to an attachment. We want ownership, we seek complete control, which in turn leads to jealousy.

Each one of these six enemies are capable of causing an immense amount of discomfort and pain, and it takes effort to overcome every one of the Arishadvargas. Sometimes, in overcoming one, we get more involved in another. For example, if we acquire control over our anger and jealousy, we start feeling pride in ourselves and when we give up attachment at times, it can lead to anger and feelings of jealousy. This is probably why it is said in the Vedas that one who has overcome all the Arishadvargas has earned the title of a wise person and now possesses the ability to go further in his spiritual quest. This battle against the six enemies has to be won effectively in the Swadisthana Chakra.

The Swadisthana Chakra is depicted as a six-petalled lotus which symbolises the six enemies of the mind we just discussed. Inside the lotus, we see a white/ silver crescent moon which stands both as a symbol of Shakti, the feminine aspect of creation, and also the water element. As we all know, the ocean ebbs and tides along with the moon, and a woman's body is also instinctively in tune with the various phases of the moon as it aligns its cycles with the moon's waxing and waning.

The crocodile is the animal symbol of this Chakra, representing a lazy and pernicious reptile that lies dormant but unleashes immense power and vitality when awakened, much like how the energy in this Chakra can become active and agile once aroused.

The fundamental quality of this Chakra is the sense of self. We may not be aware of it but we all have a sense of personal identity that goes beyond our name, position and work that we do. How we think about ourselves is largely developed over time from infancy until adulthood and continues to remain fluid, going through changes from time to time. Our experiences during childhood play an important role in how we perceive ourselves, and this is developed partly by the feedback we receive from our parents, siblings, teachers and society in general.

Ilene Strauss Cohen writes in *Psychology Today*: "Knowing yourself and becoming confident in who you are isn't as easy as it may sound. Building a strong sense of yourself can seem like an impossible task at times. It's a lifelong project figuring out who you are, what you value, and what is important to you. It is especially hard to know yourself when living in a culture that sends us constant messages about who we should be and what we should like. It makes it challenging for us to separate what we want from what other people want. It is hard to know ourselves and find our own voice in the midst of so many other dominant ideas and opinions."

A strong sense of self is essential in taking control of your own life and to help you in setting boundaries to ensure that you remain in control. An increased awareness of one's sense of self reduces stress considerably while also helping you come to terms with your relationship with the world at large. It gives you the ability to identify your own strengths, weakness and put yourself first in an unselfish fashion.

The Swadisthana Chakra is associated with the sense of taste. Taste is the perception produced or stimulated when a substance in the mouth reacts chemically with the taste receptor cells located on the taste buds in the oral cavity, mostly on the tongue. Through the tongue flows the water element of saliva, which enlivens our taste buds and helps us differentiate between the six rasas, as delineated in Ayurveda:

- Sweet
- Salty
- Pungent
- Astringent
- Bitter
- Sour

The Bija Mantra of the Swadishtana Chakra is "Vam". This mantra resonates as a frequency that activates the pelvic region. To explore this for yourself, try chanting the word "Vam" for 4–5 minutes while focusing your attention on your pelvic region, and see if you can sense the vibrations as a tiny fluttering or mild sensations in this area.

The colour associated with this Chakra is a fiery orange, the hue of the sun. This is a colour that radiates joy and warmth, a combination of the stimulation of red with the vivacity and cheer of yellow. It is a warm and welcoming colour, which stimulates the mind and spirit. The colour orange has the second longest wavelength and second slowest frequency in the visual colour spectrum. From a spiritual standpoint, the colour is associated with two auspicious objects of Hindu mythology – the colour of the sunrise and sunset (sandhya) and the colour of fire (Agni), which represents the burning away of all impurities while also dispelling darkness and bringing in the light of knowledge in the place of ignorance. Saffron, the burnt-orange hue of the eponymous precious spice, is also the most sacred colour in Hinduism. This is the colour associated with sadhus as both Hindu and Buddhist monks wear orange to show their disengagement from the world.

Sadhguru says, "Normally, a person who switches to orange drops everything that was old – his name, his identity, his family, his looks, his everything – and shifts into a different life. That means he is making a new beginning, a new sun has risen in his life. A certain realisation has come where he is willing to shed everything and walk into another dimension of life or another possibility. It also suggests 'gnana' and vision. Either a person has developed or he wants to develop a new vision, that's why he is going into it. For both people it is good to wear orange. Orange is also a symbolism. When the sun rises in the morning, it is orange. You wear this colour to indicate that a new light has come into your life and a new rising has happened within you – a new udaya. A new sun is beginning to rise within you. Another aspect is, when the fruit matures, it becomes orange. Orange is a symbol of maturity. When a person has attained a certain level of maturity or ripening, he uses this colour."

A person with a balanced Swadisthana Chakra exhibits qualities of being emotionally grounded, a high emotional intelligence with the ability to experience pleasure without feeling a sense of guilt, adapt quickly to change, be involved in creative activities, set healthy boundaries and above all, have a keen and realistic sense of self. Physically, the person will have no difficulties in movement (no stiffness or lower back pains), will feel sexually desirable, be fertile with healthy egg and sperm. There will be no issues with sweating (either excessive or too little) and the kidneys and pancreas will work optimally. Such a person will also have a normal sex drive with no sexual dysfunctions or problems. Emotionally, the person will feel nourished by relationships and will love unconditionally.

When the Swadisthana Chakra is out of balance, the person tends to become either non-responsive or overemotional, investing too much in others or cutting off from everyone, unable to draw clear boundaries, lacking in self-esteem and sometimes enduring abusive relationships simply because of lack of self-worth.

The Swadishtana Chakra is the container of all our unconscious and unfulfilled desires, including our sexual desire. In Hindu mythology, a great deal of importance is attached to overcoming the temptation to give in to the sexual union. Celibacy is usually associated with sadhus who withdraw from society and renounce all worldly ties. Celibacy, which can loosely be termed as Brahmacharya, literally translated means "dedicated to the divinity of life". The purpose of practising Brahmacharya is to keep a person focused on the purpose in life without being distracted by pleasures of the flesh.

In the Vedas, it is said that sexual passion when channelled rightly through Brahmacharya will manifest as devotion. Devotion can then be further channelled to manifest as a spiritual experience. Some Hindu schools of thought propound Brahmacharya as a necessary path for spiritual growth while others, such as Tantra philosophy, holds the contrary view that even sexual union can be used as a means to experience divinity. It is this belief that had led to the explosion of the idea of "Tantric sex", especially in the West where there is no understanding of the essential nature of Tantra.

Swami Satyananda Saraswati explains that eventually the choice to be celibate or not depends entirely on the practitioner and that a forced suppression can do more harm than good. He says, "Sexual relationships are not a sin, but the consciousness must awaken and the purpose of the whole act must be transmuted...If you think that to be a yogi you must give up sex, why don't you also give up eating and sleeping? Yoga has nothing to do with giving up these things; it is only concerned with transforming their purpose and meaning."

Ask yourself the following questions to understand the functioning of your own Swadisthana Chakra:

- Have I suffered from any traumatic early childhood or adult life experiences?
- Have I experienced body shaming at any point in my life?
- Have I been a victim of any form of abuse – emotional or physical?
- Did I have a very strict, authoritarian upbringing?
- Have I been in toxic relationships repeatedly?
- Do I feel that my sex drive is not normal (you often feel frigid or you find yourself obsessing about sex)?
- Do I suffer from any form of addiction (to work, liquor, drugs, nicotine, sex)?

Here are a few signs that you may be experiencing an imbalance in the Swadisthana Chakra:

- You feel an obsession with sensations and pleasure
- You feel uncomfortable in the presence of the opposite sex
- You generally feel ashamed when you think of sex
- You are constantly restless and suffer from anxiety and depression
- You do not feel comfortable in a social set-up, i.e., don't feel connected with people
- You feel a sense of blockage with regard to creativity
- You feel envy and jealousy
- You find yourself overly concerned about your status and make constant efforts to appear important or famous
- You have issues with low back pain, PCOS and infertility
- You suffer from kidney stones, gall bladder infections, impotence and UTI frequently

Typically, if there is a blockage or if the energy in this Chakra is not free flowing, it shows up as fatigue, diminished desire to interact with others, feelings of detachment, lack of emotional warmth and sexual frigidity. On the other hand, excessive energy in this Chakra can be seen as clingy emotional behaviour, angry outbursts, sexual addictions and inability to remain in faithful and meaningful relationships.

Here are some of the best Swadisthana Chakra healing practices:

Acceptance

Accept yourself unconditionally and clear all self-doubt that you may have by understanding that there is no human who is perfect. We are all born with shortcomings and limitations and this life is an opportunity provided to us to overcome our own sense of inadequacy and to accept that we are just as we ought to be. The world will always make efforts to hack our self-esteem, and it is up to us to not let anyone or any situation have this power over us.

Take Responsibility

Take full responsibility for your life by acknowledging that your present situation is entirely of your own making. You cannot blame your parents, teachers or society for how you turned out as a person. They all played their role as best as they could, possibly with the best intentions, but in the final run-up, understand that you are the sum total of your Karmas and the sooner you accept responsibility, the faster you can move in your spiritual quest.

Play

Indulge in what really makes you happy by using your creativity regularly. You may be a very busy professional but take time out to "play" and involve yourself in something that you do not see as "work". It could be cooking, gardening, writing, photography, painting or any activity that makes you feel fulfilled while activating your creative juices.

Respect and Honour Your Body

Respect and honour your body by taking good care of not just the physical body but also paying attention to the needs of your mind and spirit. One way of honouring your body and mind is by making sure you get adequate exercise, sufficient nutrition and by managing stress. For the well-being of the spirit, you will need to keep aside some time to contemplate the meaning of life and involve yourself in some form of prayer, meditation, satsang or even just alone-time to process your own inner feelings and emotions.

Healthy Relationships

Maintain a healthy sex life with one partner whom you trust and feel truly connected to; resist the temptation to indulge in empty, casual sexual relations which only add unnecessary emotional baggage. Honour your partner by staying faithful in thought and action and if at some point you feel the connection no longer exists, then call off the relationship in a mature fashion and do not allow bitterness to creep in.

Proximity to Water

Spend time near water bodies like lakes, rivers or oceans and also use any opportunity that may arise to swim or use a steam, sauna, hot tub, etc.

Left Nostril Breathing

Practice left nostril breathing (also known as Ida Nadi breathing). The Ida is associated with lunar energy and this helps to strengthen it further. Close your right nostril with two fingers of your right hand and inhale and exhale only through the left nostril for up to 10 breaths. Slowly with practice, you can take it up to 15 breaths.

Explore the Root of Your Addictions

What is it that makes you feel the need for adding something to your life to make it seem complete? Why do you reach out for that drink or cigarette? How does it make you feel? Empowered? Fulfilled? Complete? Why? Where does you own self feel incomplete? Is it rooted in some childhood memory or is this something you experienced as an adult? Did you feel rejection as a child? Are you trying to compensate for this by seeking out multiple sexual partners who will make you feel wanted? Ask yourself these questions until you are able to find the answers for yourself and possibly you will get control over your addiction as well.

Aromatherapy

Use aromatherapy oils such as ginger, neroli, bergamot and orange. These aromas which are warming in nature will help to bring about a balance in this Chakra.

Yoga

Asanas which involve activation of the pelvic region are very useful in balancing the Swadisthana Chakra. Some asanas which you can practice include:

- Goddess Squat: Utkata Konasana
- Fish Pose: Matsyasana
- Butterfly pose: Baddha konasana
- Cobra pose: Bhujangasana
- Two-Footed pose: Dvipada Pitham
- Legs Up the Wall pose: Viparita Karini

Use these affirmations when you are feeling particularly vulnerable:

- I honour and respect my body
- I am fulfilled and content in myself
- I am filled with self-esteem
- I allow myself to feel my emotions
- I am creative

- I value my own sexuality
- I approach sex as a sacred act

Chanting

Chant "Vam". Rest your hands in your lap with the palms facing upwards, on top of each other. Focus your thoughts on the Swadishtana Chakra and chant while visualising a bright orange vortex of light spinning rapidly in the region below your belly button.

Kati Basti

Kati Basti, an Ayurveda treatment which involves application and retention of warm oil on the lower back, is very useful in helping this Chakra heal.

The lesson of the Swadisthana Chakra is that all the fears and obstacles we experience are within us. It is only in looking inwards that we can find the answers to all our questions. No outside agency can give us the answers or help us find enlightenment. Every person who has found salvation has achieved it only upon his/her own work. We have now moved from the darkness and ignorance of the unconscious Muladhara Chakra to the beginnings of the glimmers of light as seen in the subconscious Swadisthana. No doubt, it is a scary experience as we question ourselves deeply and arrive at answers which lie embedded in our past. We are digging up old emotional wounds and setting them free from our cellular memories. These wounds have also left their imprints in our energy body and our incessant raking will help to bring about a release and free us from the tight grip of the past. With the Swadisthana Chakra now slowly coming into a balanced state, you will find yourself blossoming as a person. You will lose the fear of failure, be willing to take calculated risks and make full use of your creative urges. You will start to become more and more comfortable in your own skin, no longer struggling with issues of self-esteem and self-worth. You will find happiness in healthy, stable and joyous relationships and be open to exploring all the sensuous pleasures that life has to offer with renewed passion and zest.

8

MANIPURA CHAKRA
THE GUT-BRAIN AXIS

"Tis in ourselves that we are thus or thus. Our bodies are our gardens to the which our wills are gardeners."

– William Shakespeare

The earth's core forms the hot, dense centre of our planet. The ball-shaped core lies beneath the cool, brittle crust and the mostly solid mantle. In much the same way, the glowing yellow Manipura Chakra ("mani" meaning "gem or jewel" and "pura" meaning "city", thus giving rise to the "City of Gems") constitutes the core of our bodies, suffusing our energy with heat, light and power. We have now surpassed the unconscious and subconscious realms of the Muladhara and Swadisthana Chakra to arrive at the activation site of the ignition of consciousness.

In the Tantric tradition, the Muladhara Chakra is seen as the seat of the Kundalini with Swadisthana serving as its abode. For most people, the Kundalini keeps flitting between the bottom two Chakras because they are unable to transcend the six enemies of the mind that are encountered at the Swadisthana. It is for this reason that the Kundalini rising to the Manipura Chakra is seen as a "true awakening" from where there is no looking back on the path of spiritual ascension. Consciousness has managed to work its way through the density of Earth energy and overcome Karma in the turgid Water energy to burn through the Fire energy of this Chakra and move to higher areas of consciousness as we are able to discern truth from illusion.

The Manipura Chakra represents the Fire (Agni) element which is hot, sharp, light, penetrating, luminous and clear. The Fire element is manifested as heat in both body and mind; in the body, this heat is responsible for the digestive fire or "Agni" while it regulates control over our willpower in the mind. Agni, the digestive fire, is responsible for "paka" (digestion and transformation) as ingested food goes through the process of absorption, assimilation and distribution to various parts of the body.

In Ayurveda, Agni is crucial for the maintenance of overall health. Agni is the force of intelligence within each cell, each tissue and every system within the body. Ultimately, it is the discernment of Agni that determines which substances enter our cells and tissues, and which substances should be removed as waste. In this way, Agni is the gatekeeper of life. In fact, when Agni is extinguished, death soon follows.

Agni is divided into 13 types, based on functions and site of action.

- Jatharagni which digests and transforms food

- Bhutagni which are of five types, acting on respective portions of food and nourishing the bhutas of the body
- Dhatvagni which are of seven types, acting on the respective seven dhatus.

The entire process of the transformation of food leads to two products – prasada (essence) and kitta (excreta). While prasada provides nourishment to the body, kitta needs to be periodically removed from the body to avert it from turning toxic.

In Indian culture, a great deal of importance is placed on the food that we consume – not just what we eat but also how it is procured, how it is cooked and how it is consumed. The reason for this attention to detail is because all food carry frequency-based messages and have the ability to change our vibrations. We are told that we should not eat food which is cooked by someone who may have a reason to despise us, that we must be cheerful and peaceful while cooking food (not angry or resentful) and we must eat in silence while sitting down without any distractions. There is also the debate about vegetarian versus non-vegetarian food.

What we eat eventually becomes part of our being and like pretty much everything else in the Universe, food is also imbued with prana. The endeavour in Ayurveda is to eat food that is rich in prana, throbbing with live energy rather than to eat food that offer nothing but empty calories.

Food high in prana include

- freshly picked fruits and vegetables which are consumed as close to the source of production as possible
- Sprouted food which evoke the living energy through the process of germination
- Spices such as ginger, turmeric, cloves, cinnamon
- Cold-pressed oils such as sesame oil, coconut oil and olive oil
- Nuts and seeds – especially almonds which are soaked in water for a few hours
- Seasonal fruits and vegetables

Food that are very low in prana include:

- Fruits and vegetables that have travelled a long distance
- Genetically modified food
- Frozen food
- Food made using hydrogenated oils
- Anything cooked in a microwave oven
- Non-vegetarian food

It is very important for our own well-being to pay a little attention to what we consume. We must attempt to eat food with high prana whenever possible, knowing that it is impractical to go seeking such food at all times. If we are able to find a balance wherein, we are consuming healthy food at least for a major portion of the week, it will help a great deal in bringing about a better sense of well-being in us. It is also very important to eat slowly and be in a calm frame of mind. Avoid eating when you are angry or stressed as the body may not be receptive to food eaten at such times. Make a conscious effort to avoid watching television, reading or talking on the phone while eating. Treating the act of eating as a sacred ritual will ensure that there is minimum ama (toxins) left behind after the process is completed.

Paramhans Swami Maheshwara says, "It is tremendously important for both our physical and mental health that we consume healthy, energy giving food that has a pure, positive vibration. Before we eat we should find out where the food has come from and what qualities it contains. It is not only the nutrients that are important but also the subtle vibrations of the food, which have a marked effect on the body, mind and our spiritual energy. These vibrations can considerably alter our physical well-being, our thoughts, feelings and vitality. A basic question we should put to ourselves is: "Is the food we are eating connected with the pain, suffering or death of any living being?"

Physically, the Manipura Chakra is depicted as residing behind the navel, at the centre of the spine. In the physical body, the Manipura Chakra governs not only digestive and absorptive aspects but is also related to our small intestine, liver, spleen, pancreas, adrenal glands, red blood cells and eyes. With regards to our psychological make up and spiritual nature, we see its influence on our personal dynamism, willpower, sense of status and feeling of power.

The Manipura Chakra is depicted as a ten-petalled lotus. The ten petals symbolise the ten types of pranas that are regulated in this Chakra. We have already discussed the five prana-vayus (Samana, Prana, Apana, Vyana, Udana) in a previous chapter. The other five pranas are the Upa Vayus:

- Naga – the function of burping
- Kurma – the function of blinking
- Devadatta – the function of yawning
- Krikala – the function of sneezing
- Dhananjaya – the function of opening and closing heart valves

We all radiate an aura which is easily perceptible to others. This aura is a function of our Prana (all ten types of prana combined that radiates throughout our body) and is deeply connected not just with our physical well-being, internal biorhythm and immunity levels but also with our thoughts and feelings, emotions and state of mind such as anxiety, stress and negativity.

A red-coloured downward-facing triangle is also seen in the Manipura Chakra as a symbol for a flame which expands and rises upwards.

The animal symbol of the Manipura Chakra is the fiery large-horned male sheep – the Ram, an animal that lives mostly in the mountains, is famous for its hot-headedness and characterised by its desire to dominate and be the alpha-male of its brood.

The fundamental quality of this Chakra is willpower. At the core of willpower lies the ability to resist short-term temptations and desires in order to achieve long-term goals. It's the prevailing source of long-term satisfaction over instant gratification, writes Catarina Lino in *The Psychology of Willpower*. She adds that we rely on willpower to exercise, diet, save money, quit smoking, stop drinking, overcome procrastination, and ultimately accomplish any of our goals. It impacts every area of our lives. Studies show that when compared to more impulsive individuals, people scoring high on self-control are more apt at regulating behavioural, emotional and attention impulses to achieve long-term goals.

Psychologist Kelly McGonigal calls willpower the "I won't power. The biggest enemies of willpower are temptation, self-criticism and stress. Three skills – self-awareness, self-care and remembering what matter most – are the foundation for self-control." Willpower is seen as one of the key determinants of both personal and professional success. Willpower is what helps us create lasting positive changes in our lives. It is the inner strength helping us move toward our goals despite inevitable challenges. Dan Millman says, "Willpower is the key to success. Successful people strive no matter what they feel by applying their will to overcome apathy, doubt or fear."

The Manipura Chakra is associated with our sense of sight. Our eyes are the sense organs that act as a collector of light, giving us sight. The delicate structure of the eyes enables entering light energy to be converted to electrochemical energy. This stimulates the visual centres in the brain, giving us the sensation of seeing.

It is not merely the sense of sight but also "insight" that is governed by this Chakra. We speak of "gut instinct" when we just know intuitively that something is wrong or that something will work for us. The gut is very closely connected to the brain via nerve bundles, often informing the brain about what emotions it should feel. This is the reason why the gut is often referred to as the "second brain". The main channel of communication between the gut and the brain is known as the "gut–brain axis". The two primary nerve divisions – the Vagus nerve and the solar plexus are responsible for messages that are conveyed between the gut and the brain, and they converge at the Manipura Chakra.

This connection is crucial for the mind–body association and for many of the systems that operate within the body. It has an effect on our overall health and well-being, immunity and stress response.

Recent studies have shown that some cells in the organs of the digestive system produce serotonin – an important neurotransmitter linked to good feelings such as happiness, contentment and calmness. If the body does not produce sufficient amount of serotonin, it leads to anxiety, stress and depression. A large portion of the serotonin produced by the body is made and found in the gut. Our digestive system, therefore, not only sustains us but is also largely responsible for how we feel.

The Bija Mantra of the Manipura Chakra is "Ram".

The colour associated with this Chakra is a bright cheery yellow (much like the colour of a sunflower). Yellow, occurring between orange and green on the spectrum, can be bright and intense, which is why it can often invoke strong feelings. Yellow can also arouse feelings of frustration and anger, and studies have shown that people are more likely to lose their tempers in yellow rooms and babies tend to cry more in places where there is a preponderance of yellow.

An individual with a balanced Manipura Chakra exhibits a personality that is cheerful, healthy and equanimous. He has formed good food habits (not prone to overeating or denying himself food), has healthy digestion with good metabolism, has excellent eyesight and most of all, is able to rely on his gut instinct to make the right decisions.

When the Manipura Chakra is out of balance because of deficiency or excess energy, it manifests as digestive disorders such as Irritable Bowel Syndrome, Crohn's Disease, Gastric Reflux, bloating, constipation and an overall feeling of fatigue and malaise. Diabetes is also associated with the malfunctioning of this Chakra as the pancreas is governed by this energy centre.

In the mind, this imbalance is seen as an acute lack of willpower, with a desire for instant gratification in all aspects of life (whether it is food, sex or material belongings).

Ask yourself the following questions to arrive at a better understanding of your Manipura Chakra:

- Do I often feel powerless or victimised?
- Do I give my power away to others in order to keep peace in relationships?
- Do I have difficulty in acting on my dreams because I lack self-esteem?
- Do I trust my intuition and have faith in my inner guIdance?

- Do I constantly feel the need in other people's confirmation and valIdation?
- Do I find ways to shame myself?
- Do I suffer from indigestion, heartburn or anxiety?

Here are a few signs that you may be experiencing an imbalance in the Manipura Chakra:

- You feel lazy, passive and uninterested
- You are constantly tired and feel fatigue often
- You are frequently seen as a bully or as a dominating person
- You suffer from stomach pains, bloating and allergies
- You have ulcers
- You are a diabetic
- You often feel unable to assert yourself in situations
- You cannot take decisions based on your inner guIdance
- You seek information excessively to help you arrive at decisions

Here are some of the best Manipura Chakra healing practices:

Make a Conscious Effort to Heal from the Past

Our past trauma lingers on at the cellular level and continues to affect our thoughts and actions on a subconscious level. Those who have been raised in authoritarian or rigid households will need to make a great effort to overcome the conditioning of their past. Physical wounds heal much more easily than mental ones. You will need to find ways to forgive others and more importantly, also forgive yourself to free your being from the bondage of these past, often-repressed memories.

Define Yourself and Your Life's Purpose

Your life purpose is the one recurring theme or idea that exemplifies your main life goals. "It is the specific way in which you engage with life that makes use of all that you are and draws on your unique experiences, talents, abilities and interests in a way that helps you achieve your highest goals while being of service to others," says Kathy Caprino in a Forbes article[2]. She goes on to add that to identify your life purpose, connect the dots from your childhood onward to discover who you have always been. This exercise does make a positive difference in people's lives.

Respond Positively to Criticism from Others

Personal and professional success depend to a large extent on your ability to take criticism in your stride. Criticism can be irrelevant, destructive or constructive. If you find yourself at the receiving end of irrelevant criticism, it is best to ignore it. If you find that someone has an opinion that could be destructive, you could open a channel of dialogue without attaching too much importance to it and keeping in mind that there may be some agenda at play. If the criticism is constructive, then it would be best taken as a life lesson.

Build Self-Discipline and Engage Your Willpower

Overcome the urge for instant gratification and start looking at what long-term benefits you can accrue from short-term sacrifices. This can apply to some or all walks of life, whether it is about saying no to that delicious samosa or that extra drink at the club. Set yourself clear goals so that you can stick to them more easily.

Learn from Life's Difficulties

Failure is an inevitable part of life. If you haven't failed at anything yet, then you have not tried something new. We learn much more from failure than we will ever know from success. Use every obstacle in your path as a learning. Also keep in mind that failure and fault are virtually inseparable in most households, organisations and cultures. Every child learns at some point that admitting failure means taking the blame, says Amy Edmondson in the Harvard Business Review. So, start taking blame

---

[2] https://www.forbes.com/sites/kathycaprino/2018/11/28/three-simple-steps-to-identify-your-life-purpose-and-leverage-it-in-your-career/#2da6e293695f

and face up to the responsibility that you and you alone are the reason for how your life is turning out.

Let Go of Unhealthy Attachments

Unhealthy attachments cause a tremendous loss of energy and are very often responsible for blocks and stagnation. Attachments can be emotional, mental or physical. We can get attached in an unhealthy manner to not just people or places but to our ideas, beliefs, prejudices, desires, fears and objects. These attachments will need to be released in order to stop energy leakage.

Take Up a New Hobby

Try some activities which stimulate the mind and sharpen your instinct. Try instinct-based games to develop your trust in your inner guidance system.

Food

Favour food such as lemon, bananas, yellow capsicum, corn, turmeric. Yellow food is rich in an antioxidant called lutein.

Aromatherapy

Arouse your sense of personal power using scents which have a fiery base such as oud, sandalwood, musk, black pepper, ginger and cinnamon.

Sun Exposure

The sun can be a huge source of vitality and health and this is particularly important in the case of the Manipura Chakra as its element is fire.

Use Affirmations

* I honour the power within me
* I acknowledge my inner guide

* I am capable of fulfilling my dreams
* I am worthy of respect
* I possess willpower
* I forgive others and myself
* I nourish my body and mind with the right food
* I feel strong at the core of my being

Yoga

Asanas will help strengthen the core and balance the Manipura Chakra. These include:

* Boat Pose: Navasana
* Cat Pose: Marjaryasana
* Chair Pose: Utkatasana
* Crow Pose: Bakasana
* Side plank pose: Vasisthasana
* Half-moon pose: Ardha Chandrasana
* Eagle pose: Garudasana

Chakra Basti

An Ayurveda therapy called Chakra Basti, which involves application and retention of warm oil on the stomach region, is very useful in helping this Chakra heal.

Chant "Ram"

While visualising a bright yellow spinning ball of light in your solar plexus region, chant "Ram" either mentally or loudly and focus on removing any stains, blots, blocks that you may encounter in your mental visual until you see a throbbing, pulsating bright light of yellow.

The Manipura Chakra or the "City of Gems" has been aptly named by our ancient seers as it denotes the luminous fire that burns at the core of our being where the mind and body come together to form a strong connection. Here, we are almost half way through the journey of the Kundalini from Muladhara to Sahasrara Chakra. The lustre generated in this "City of Gems" radiates to both the lower and higher Chakras – feelings of happiness, love and well-being originate here and find expression in the Anahata Chakra, while the same positive feelings purify and strengthen the Swadisthana and Muladhara Chakras.

Fire can be destructive when it is not controlled and in the same way, the fire of the Manipura Chakra can lead to passion, restlessness and aggressive behaviour. When we have full control over this fire element, we can use it as a means of purification and refinement. We can allow the fire to burn away all that which is not serving us anymore, and purify our own actions and intentions.

A strong, balanced and harmonious Manipura Chakra guarantees that you will feel confident in the decisions that you take while offering you a sense of autonomy and heightened desire for action. You will feel energised, focused, empowered, and in alignment with life. This Chakra is the Pranic hub, sustaining all tissues and stoking the fires necessary to keep the physiological process moving smoothly. We can only feel fully healthy and vital when we are able to digest not merely the food that we ingest but also break down, absorb and assimilate all aspects of reality that we experience in our lives.

9

ANAHATA CHAKRA
OUR INNER TEMPLE OF LOVE

"And now here is my secret, a very simple secret: It is only with the heart that one can see rightly; what is essential is invisible to the eye."

– Antoine de Saint-Exupéry, *The Little Prince*

We have now moved from the steady groundedness of the Earth element in the Muladhara Chakra, through the fluid, creative element of Water in the Swadisthana Chakra to the transformational heat of the Fire energy in the Manipura Chakra to arrive at the Anahata Chakra, which is dominated by Air energy. This Chakra forms the basis for movement and expansion, while symbolising the breadth and boundlessness of the heart within which our consciousness is able to expand without restriction. We are now at the Heart Chakra where the "Jivatma" or individual soul is said to reside. It is in this Chakra that we learn the valuable lesson that love is the reason for our existence. Not love in the romantic sense of the word but love as an all-encompassing, ever-expanding quality that overwhelms us as we understand our deep interconnectedness with every atom in the Universe.

We use the expression "heart" to signify the centre of something, as in "the heart of the matter" or "at the heart of the concept". In our bodies, the heart is seen as the centre, not just of our physical being but also of our mental and spiritual identity. In the *Taittiriya* and *Chandogya Upanishads*, we come across the term "hridaya guha" or heart cave where Universal Consciousness resides. "Go into the cave and you find the treasures of heaven," says the *Chhandogya Upanishad*, going on to add "the sun and the moon and the stars, the very space and the clouds and the lightning and the rains – all this miracle of creation is within the heart of man. When it rains outside, it rains inside also, and the stellar regions shine resplendently within the heart of man."

Anahata in Sanskrit means "unstruck sound". We understand sound as a result of two objects touching to create a vibration that can be heard. Examples of such sound include two palms coming together to clap, drum beats produced when a stick beats a leather surface or when two cymbals come together to produce a noise. In contrast, Anahata is a primordial sound – the eternal, unborn and undying vibration, the pulse of the Universe which is produced without two parts coming in contact. Anahata refers to the possibility that arises at this Chakra for two opposing forces to come together without a confrontational outcome. In other words, it is possible to integrate two opposing forces and bring about a peaceful, cooperative and cohesive outcome.

The Anahata Chakra represents the Air (Vayu) element which is mobile, cool, light, dry, subtle, flowing and sharp. The air element is manifested as circulation in the body with the heart at its centre. In the body, it is responsible for the maintenance of blood pressure, respiration and movement of hands, while it regulates the dispersion and integration of spiritual understanding in the mental and spiritual plane.

In Ayurveda, Air is related to the Pancha Prana (five pranas), and Vedic texts relate the energy in the Anahata Chakra to both the Prana Vayu (which is to be understood as the secondary "prana", not the primary life giving one) that regulates respiration and to Vyana Vayu which relates to the distribution and communication systems of the body. While Prana Vayu is an inward energy, Vyana is an outward one, and both these come together at this Chakra to make breath, and therefore, life itself possible.

Physically, the Anahata Chakra is depicted as residing to the right of the physical heart, almost at the centre of our thoracic cavity. In the physical body, the Chakra governs the heart, thymus, immune system, lungs, breasts, arms and hands. In our psychological make up, the Chakra is responsible for our feelings of love, compassion, empathy and connectedness with the rest of the world.

The Anahata Chakra is depicted as a twelve-petalled lotus. The twelve petals symbolise the twelve "vrittis" or divine qualities of the heart: joy, peace, love, harmony, bliss, clarity, purity, compassion, understanding, forgiveness, patience and kindness.

William Enckhausen defines half of these vrittis as spiritual ignorances and half as spiritual developments. "Half of the 12 vrittis of the Anahata are 'positive', growth-promoting vrittis and the other half are 'negative' or at most neutral, self-justifying defence tendencies that perpetuate the ego's limited boundaries instead of expanding and refining them. There is still a limited and bounded sense of self, but with the potential to discriminate between vice and virtue. There is also still the boundary of self and not self to be overcome, although not as marked as in the Manipura and Swadisthana. Harmony, balance, and proportion are key elements in this fulcrum that is the Anahata to help determine what is growth-promoting and virtuous (self, or good for the self) and what is vice, or inappropriate for spiritual self-growth (not self)."

Within the twelve-petalled lotus lies a six-pointed star made up of two intersecting triangles – one upward facing and the other downward facing. The six points of the star are a symbol of air which moves in all four directions as well as upward and downward.

The upward-pointing triangle represents Shiva, symbolising the energy that offers us the possibility of raising our state of consciousness, while the downward-facing one is symbolic of Shakti, carrying the subtle implication that it is very easy to slip back into the lower Chakras. The two triangles facing upward and downward also depict that the Anahata Chakra serves as the gateway between basic survival-oriented impulses of the three Chakras which lie below it and the spiritual aspirations of the three Chakras that lie above it. The intersecting triangles could also symbolise the eternal inner struggle that takes place in the heart between spirituality and emotion.

A new moon in the form of a crescent is seen lying between the six-pointed star and the lotus petals, signifying that just as the moon influences all of Nature, it also exerts its influence on the heart, waxing and waning through joy and despair, through pain and comfort, through spirituality and attachment.

The animal symbol of the Anahata Chakra is a black gazelle. The gazelle is a thin, graceful antelope belonging to the same family as goats, cattle and sheep. They can run at a great speed as they have several predators in the jungle. The gazelle has to be hyper vigilant at all times of day and night in order to remain alive. In the same way, this Chakra reminds us that we need to always maintain vigil and keep a watch for predatory thoughts that arise in our own minds.

Our heart and brain are intricately connected by several neural pathways that resemble the alignment of neurons in the brain, but this axis is much more powerful and this is possibly the reason why the heart is often referred to as a "second brain", sending more feedback signals back to the brain than it receives. The heart is said to be five thousand times more powerful magnetically than the brain. A recent article in *Gaia* titled *Mysteries of the Human Heart,* it says "neurons, the brain cells responsible for processing sense-based input, send messages to the body such as 'reach hand to pick up sandwich'. Neurons also transmit emotion. These specialised cells are found in the brain and nervous system but more importantly, also in the heart. Neurons can be harnessed to establish heart–brain coherence – in fact, heart neurons fire in conjunction with the brain neurons. The heart and brain are undisputedly, profoundly connected."

Rollin McCraty, one of the founders of Heartmath, writes that an important key to our well-being is creating currents or pathways of brain–heart coherence. A new field of study called neurocardiology confirms the ancient wisdom around the power of our innate intelligence and our inherent ability to sync with the wisdom of our heart–brain to empower pathways of well-being. Through neuroplasticity, these pathways lead to patterns of resonance and alignment within our heart/mind intelligence. She shares that "the biggest hidden source of stress on the planet is the disorganisation of heart/mind, causing a lack of resonance. Lack of alignment eats the life force and happiness out of humanity."

The fundamental quality of this Chakra is love. The human heart has long been associated with emotion and pleasure – the shape seen as a symbol of love. Among the earliest known examples is the Greek poet Sappho who agonised over her own "mad heart" quaking with love writing, "Love shook my heart, Like the wind on the mountain troubling the oak-trees." Greek philosophers agreed that the heart was linked to our strongest emotions, including love. Plato discussed the dominant role of the chest in love and in experiencing negative emotions of fear, anger, rage and pain. Aristotle expanded the role of the heart even further, granting it supremacy in all human processes.

The ancient Romans held a curious belief about the heart – that there was a vein extending from the fourth finger of the left hand directly to the heart. They called it the vena amoris. Even though this idea was based upon incorrect knowledge of the human anatomy, it persisted and in the medieval period, the groom was told to place a ring on the bride's fourth finger because of that vein. Josh Hartnell explains that they also inherited the Greek idea that the heart was the first organ your body made, and hence, the one that most anchored your human existence – it was the "house of the human soul".

Love encompasses a range of strong emotional and mental states – both positive and negative. While love in its positive state is seen as a virtue which brings about connectedness, caring, concern and benevolence, the same affection has the potential to turn into a vice when it takes the form of obsessiveness, vanity, selfishness and undue attachment. Love in its positive state has been described by various philosophers as providing the main motivation for human life and facilitating the continuation of the species. Greek philosophers identified five forms of love:

- Familial love (Storge)
- Friendly or platonic love (Philia)
- Romantic love (Eros)
- Guest love (Xenia)
- Divine love (Agape)

Helen Fisher, an anthropologist, divides the experience of love into three (partly overlapping) stages of lust, attraction and attachment. Lust and attraction are temporary states while attachment is a long-term connection established with the setting up of a life together, including having children, building a home and securing the future jointly. Three distinct neural circuitries, including different neurotransmitters, are associated with each of these three stages of love.

However, the love that we refer to as expressed in the Anahata Chakra is an all-encompassing Universal Love which focuses on benevolence and has its basis in duty, action and attitude, rather than in a relationship. The vibrations of this Chakra represent a transition of attention from our self, our needs, our desires to a compassion for others, their needs and their well-being. This profound leap in our evolutionary growth awakens along with intuition and spiritual consciousness. Our hearts opening up to Universal Love brings us to recognise our Self in every living being. Their pain becomes our pain just as their pleasure is felt as our own. It is only when this all-embracing love for everything around us is awakened that we can truly claim to have opened up our Anahata Chakra. Bhakti Yoga prescribes nine practices for cultivation of this Universal Love:

- Satsang: the right (spiritual) company
- Harikatha: listening to spiritual tales
- Shradda: having faith
- Bhajan: singing devotional songs
- Mantra japa: chanting of mantras
- Shama dama: exercising internal and external controls
- Santon ka adar: honouring spiritually evolved people
- Santosha: experiencing contentment at all times
- Ishwarapranidhana: surrendering to the Divine

Another important lesson that the Anahata Chakra teaches us is self-care. The heart is responsible for supplying oxygenated blood to the entire body but it does so by ensuring that its needs are met first (through the carotid artery which supplies oxygenated blood to the heart). It is only after ensuring that its needs are fulfilled that blood courses through the other arteries to the various parts of the body. The lesson from the heart Chakra is that it is imperative that we take care of ourselves and our needs first, before we venture out to fulfil the needs of others and start dispensing love and care. If we do not love or nurture ourselves fully, we will remain deficient in our love and care of others as well.

In the Vedic tradition, mantra provides a channel of communication for the common man with the Divine. Our ancient seers analysed common speech patterns working through their components to reach the earliest sources. N. Krishnaswamy writes in *The Mantra* that the rishis reasoned that all sounds emanate from energy and are designed for use as vehicles of meaning, and therefore, the true power of language lies in the power of its sounds. They identified certain special sounds as Bija Akshara or seed letters from which grosser sounds of language proliferated. Bija Akshara are sounds where meanings may not be apparent but their power and role as communication are deeply embedded in the sound itself. It is in the Anahata Chakra that we can awaken our Mantra Shakti or the power of mantras.

The most powerful method of chanting mantras is known as Ajapa Japa, which dates back to the Upanishads and stands out amongst all yogic practices as it combines meditation, mantra chanting and pranayama. Ked Suri, Founder of the Yogi Press, writes that Ajapa Japa translates to "the awareness and experience of the mantra" until the mantra comes to life and forms a part of the individual's consciousness. The most common mantras used in Ajapa Japa include Om, Sohum, the Gayatri Mantra and the Mahamrityunjaya Mantra.

Just below the Anahata Chakra lies another minor Chakra called the Hrida or Surya Chakra, which is depicted with eight petals amidst which nestles the Kalpavriksha or the Wish Fulfilling Tree. The Kalpavriksha symbolises every human's inherent ability to manifest their desires. Activating the Anahata Chakra will also result in the activation of the HrIda Chakra, thereby fulfilling desires and helping in their manifestation.

The Anahata Chakra is associated with our sense of touch. Air energy or Vayu is related physically to the skin, our organ of touch, and emotionally to our thoughts and feelings. When we are moved by something, we say "we are touched" because it is the emotional equivalent of the actual feeling of being physically touched.

The Bija Mantra of the Anahata Chakra is "Yam".

The colour associated with this Chakra is a brilliant emerald green. From ancient times, green has signified growth, rebirth and fertility. It is universally associated with Nature and symbolises ecology and the environment. The heart is often compared to a tree as it converts carbon dioxide inhaled through the breath and supplies oxygenated blood to the entire body.

A person with a balanced Anahata Chakra is open, friendly, compassionate, with unconditional love and deep compassion for self and all living beings on the planet. On the physical plane, he has a properly functioning heart and lungs while enjoying good immunity and has strong arms and capable hands.

When the Chakra is out of balance because of a blockage, deficiency or excess energy, it manifests in the physical body as high or low blood pressure, arrhythmia, arterial blocks, poor circulation, stiff joints, diminished sense of touch and less strength in arms and hands. In the mind, it shows up as feelings of hatred, mistrust, fear, and the person lacks compassion and empathy for his fellow beings. At the level of the spirit, we see it as a harbinger of bitter relationships, obsessive stalking behaviour and a constant tussle between the mind and the heart.

Ask yourself the following questions to arrive at a better understanding of your Anahata Chakra:

1. Do I find myself dwelling too much on the past?
2. Am I overly critical of myself and others?
3. Do I hold grudges?
4. Do I feel suspicious and fearful in relationships?
5. Do I have commitment issues?
6. Do I focus too much on others and not enough on myself?
7. Do I face trouble with giving and receiving love and being compassionate?
8. Do I find that I am too guarded in friendships and relationships?

Here are a few signs that you may be experiencing an imbalance in the Anahata Chakra:

- You feel like you have to please others to be loved
- You are pushing people away
- You feel anxious and stressed
- You are holding on to past pains and memories
- You tend to keep your emotions bottled up
- You tend to be needy in your relationships
- You see yourself as a martyr
- You suffer from social anxiety
- You are withdrawn and try to avoid socializing with people
- You have issues with the heart, lung or chest region such as asthma, high blood pressure or poor blood circulation
- You often feel a sense of heaviness in your chest

Here are some of the best Anahata Chakra healing practices:

Practice Heart Coherence

Of late, there has been a great deal of research on heart coherence, with studies showing that when we cultivate (intentionally or unintentionally) emotions of appreciation, love and compassion (as opposed to anxiety, anger or fear), the oscillations of our heart rhythm are more coherent or consistent. This coherence is linked to a sense of well-being, with greater emotional stability. Heart coherence is a term that describes a highly efficient psycho-physiological state in which the nervous system, cardiovascular, hormonal and immune systems are working together efficiently and harmoniously.

The pattern of heart rhythm reflects the state of emotions we feel. For example, the heart rhythm is disordered and incoherent when we are feeling tense, fearful, anxious or stressed. The heart signals "incoherence" to the brain, which in turn triggers the stress response-producing hormones such as adrenaline and cortisol, resulting in elevated heart rate, shallow breathing, sweating, etc. Positive emotions, on the other hand, send coherent signals to the brain, which then triggers the pleasure response and produces hormones such as dopamine, endorphin and oxytocin. These are related to feelings of joy, peace and calmness. You can practice heart coherence by focusing your attention on your heart and observing the heartbeat without judgement or by imagining your breath as flowing through the heart region while visualising your heart energy expand to fill the entire space around you.

Let Go of Attachment

We all desire happiness and want to avoid pain, but inevitably we find ourselves in situations that cause us unhappiness and pain. This is largely because we depend on external things to make us happy. We seek to find our happiness in other people, in possessions, in a variety of things that lie outside of our control. We feel so closely connected to a person that his/her actions cause us grief if they are not in keeping with our expectations. While it is true that we need to bond with people and develop close relationships, we must also be aware at all times that we cannot allow these people to exercise enough power over us to make us feel bad, angry, sad, happy or cheerful. We must develop a sense of detachment from people even closest to us. This is by no means an easy task and takes a moment-to-moment commitment to know that a false sense of attachment is complicating matters for you as well as for the other person.

Get Rid of Dependency

Dependency gives rise to expectations and demands, which when unfulfilled, lead to anger and frustration. Dependency is not merely confined to our relationship with people but also with our own personality traits such as a workaholism to get away from facing life, dependency on travel to escape everyday living or dependency on social media approvals to feel temporary self-esteem. Letting go of dependency makes us fearful and defensive as they threaten our very sense of identity.

Let Go of the Past

Marianne Williamson rightly says, "We do not heal the past by dwelling there; we heal the past by living fully in the present." We have all been hurt at some point in the past and we carry the painful memories with us throughout our life and possibly beyond. We keep reliving these painful memories and invoking the same feelings that we felt when the event occurred. The only way to stop reliving these hurts is by living fully in the present moment, allowing the memories to surface when they do, acknowledging them but bringing the mind firmly, yet gently, back to the present moment without lingering on the feelings that the memory evokes.

Stop Playing the Martyr

Playing victim feels good – we are helpless, powerless, we have no control and it is someone else's fault. It feels good because we relinquish responsibility and place the blame on others. Self-pity is addictive and separates us from reality. Blaming others may provide temporary relief, but in the long run it only leads to a deep sense of hopelessness. Get out of martyr mode by taking responsibility for your own life. Let go of feelings of bitterness and resentment and make place for positive feelings that make you feel empowered and in control.

Be Thankful and Show Gratitude

Gratitude is strongly associated with greater feelings of happiness. When we cultivate appreciation and compassion, our heart rhythm actually becomes more consistent, which is linked to a greater sense of well-being.

Do a Forgiveness Ritual

Remember that forgiveness is not about the person you are forgiving. It is all about you. It is your way of handling the pain you have felt. You can either live with it all your life, carrying its heavy burden or let go of it by transforming it into compassion, empathy and understanding. A forgiveness ritual such as the Ayurvedic Tarpana helps immensely in finding the inner strength to move beyond the pain to find peace and freedom.

Use Pranayama Techniques

As the heart Chakra is ruled by the element of air, pranayama techniques are particularly useful in bringing this Chakra into a balance. Alternative nostril breathing and other breath control exercises are highly beneficial.

Spend Time in Nature

Spending time in nature brings a feeling of serenity, peace and calm. It can improve our physical and psychological health. In the book *Your Brain On Nature: The Science of Nature's Influence on Your Health, Happiness and Vitality*, Eva M. Selhub, MD and Alan C. Logan explain that scientific studies show that natural environments can have remarkable benefits for human health. Spending just 20 minutes in vegetation-rich nature improves vitality. They define vitality as emotional strength in the face of internal and external oppositions, and living life with enthusiasm.

Aromatherapy

Essential oils that work well with the Anahata Chakra include cypress, geranium, jasmine, lavender, mandarin and neroli. Most woody scents work well to balance this Chakra.

Food

Since the colour associated with this Chakra is green, food such as spinach, cucumber, capsicum, beans, peas, avocados, raw mango, kiwi, guava and green tea are useful in bringing about a balance.

Affirmations

- I am fully open to giving and receiving love
- I am open to love
- I forgive myself and others
- I treat myself and others with compassion
- My life is filled with joy and gratitude
- I live in balance, in a state of gracefulness and gratitude
- I am grateful for all the challenges
- I am connected with other human beings
- I feel a sense of oneness with nature
- I accept things as they are
- I am peaceful

Yoga

Asanas which bring about an opening of the chest region are beneficial for this Chakra. Some of the poses are:

Camel Pose: Ushtrasana

Wheel Pose: Chakrasana

Bridge Pose: Setu Bandha Sarvangasana

Upward-facing dog pose: Urdhva Mukha Shvanasana

Bow pose: Dhanusana

Fish pose: Matsyasana

Cobra pose: Bhujangasana

Hrid Basti

A little-known Ayurveda therapy called Hrid Basti, which involves application and retention of warm oil on the chest region, is very useful in helping this Chakra heal.

Chanting

Chant "Yam" while focusing your mind on the heart region, and visualise a bright green spinning ball of light. You can also learn the Shanti Mantra, a prayer for all beings, that helps us form a deep connection with the Universe.

> Sarve Bhavantu Sukhinahah Sarve Santu Niraamayah
>
> Sarve Bhadrani Pashyantu Ma Kaschit Dukha Bhag Bhavet
>
> Om Shanti Shanti Shantih
>
> May all be happy, May all be free of sorrow
>
> May all be favoured by fortune, May no one be unhappy
>
> Om Peace Peace Peace

In Ayurveda, the heart is seen as the seat of consciousness, and as Swami Satyananda Saraswati reminds us, "although its physiological component is the cardiac plexus of nerves, the nature of this centre is far beyond the physiological dimension", it becomes vital to harmonise the heart centre so that we can learn to love ourselves and others and no longer have to struggle with feelings of isolation, anxiety, fear and anger. Opening the heart Chakra lets us release old toxic patterns as we learn to trust and love more. It helps us develop compassion and connection with the realisation that we can never advance alone while others around us are suffering. As we allow this wonderful Universal Love to pervade our being, we feel a total sense of bliss which in itself can heal a great deal of our past wounds and help us understand that Universal Love is eternal. We also realise that this Love connects us with everything else in the world and is reflected as infinite bliss as we unite with our Real Self.

10

VISHUDDHA CHAKRA
EXPRESSING OUR INNER TRUTH

"It took me quite a long time to develop a voice, and now that I have it, I am not going to be silent"

– Madeleine K. Albright

At the Anahata Chakra, we came upon the convergence of the three lower Chakras that govern our survival instinct, creativity and personal power, and the upper three Chakras that govern our spiritual ascendance with expression of our inner truth, intuitiveness and eventually, the boundlessness of enlightenment. The Anahata Chakra serves as a bridge of compassion and love which we cross from a state of selfishness (Me, me, me) to selflessness (developing empathy and compassion for all things around us). The Visuddha Chakra stands for all aspects of purification that we need to undergo as humans to be able to traverse the journey to the highest Chakra. The word "Visuddha" can be broken up into "Visha" (poison, impurity) and "Shudda" (purification), thereby symbolising a thorough cleansing of various aspects of our personality as a precursor to becoming one with our Universal Self.

The story of Samudra Manthana (churning of the ocean) is narrated in the *Mahabharata, Bhagavata* and *Vishnu Purana*. Indra, the king of Swarga, while riding his elephant Airavata comes across the learned Sage Durvasa who offers him a garland. Indra accepts the garland and places it on the trunk of his elephant. The flowers in the garland attract bees and Airavata throws the garland to the ground to get rid of the bees. This angers Sage Durvasa, who thinks it is an affront to him, and curses Indra (and thereby all the Devas), causing them to lose all their powers. The Asuras use this as an opportune moment to wage war and gain control of the Universe and are successful in doing so. At this time, the Devas approach Vishnu to help them, and Vishnu suggests that they make peace with the Asuras. The two warring groups are advised to form an alliance to seek the nectar of immortality by churning the ocean jointly.

Mount Mandara is used as the churning rod and Vasuki, the Serpent King, is used as the churning rope. The Samudra Manthana releases a potent poison called Halala which can potentially destroy all of creation. The Devas and Asuras are horrified at the imminent destruction and approach Shiva, who assumes the form of a giant tortoise and collects the poison in his throat. The poison burns his throat and leaves it permanently blue, earning him the title of Nilakantha. Shiva neither spits out the poison nor does he swallow it but purifies it in his being so that it does him (and the Universe) no harm.

This story is illustrative of the immense purificatory power of the Vishuddha Chakra. The Devas are symbols of our good qualities (love, compassion, wisdom) while the Asuras are our bad qualities (greed, anger, selfishness). The churning of the ocean is symbolic of the constant tug-of-war that takes place within each one of us between our good and bad qualities. The process of churning throws up many of our inherent qualities, just as the ocean throws up both nectar and poison. Continuing with the analogy of poison, the Vishuddha Chakra throws up two possibilities – to swallow the poison which will result in destruction of the self or to spit out the poison which may result in destroying all that which surrounds us.

Swallowing the poison is analogous to all the hurt, pain, rejection, disappointment and failure we take in from our interactions with the world without actually processing them. This creates gaping emotional and spiritual wounds that will slowly but surely spread through the body and mind, just as the poison makes its way through the body, killing cells it comes into contact with, eventually resulting in paralysis and death. Spitting the poison can be compared to our nasty and evil thoughts, hurtful words and negative actions which cause pain to others. Swallowing and spitting both take their toll on our consciousness. In the Vishuddha Chakra, Amrita (nectar) drips into the Chitrini Nadi where it divides into a poison and a pure form. Practices such as Kechari Mudra and the Jalandhara Bandha purify the poison, thus detoxifying and cleansing the body.

A minor Chakra known as Lalana is located at the roof of the mouth and is generally closely associated with the Vishuddha Chakra. It is seen as having 12 red petals that correspond to the twelve vrittis (virtues), which need to be cultivated by one seeking to grow spiritually (and have been discussed in an earlier chapter). Inside the petals lies a full moon which acts as the reservoir for the nectar Amrita. This is associated with a chemical produced by the body that supports preservation of health, youthfulness and vitality. Most often this nectar drips wastefully into the Manipura Chakra where it is burned by the digestive fire. Yogic practices, such as Kechari Mudra, can help to utilise this hormone for the well-being of the body and mind.

The Vishuddha Chakra represents the element of Ether or Space (Akasha) whose qualities are ever-expanding, vast, spacious and intangible. While Earth, Water, Fire and Air are all elements found on our planet, we now move into the realms beyond Earth as Akasha permeates the entire Universe and beyond. In this Chakra, all the elements get refined into their purest essence and become one with Akasha. In the physical body, this Chakra governs the neck, throat, jaws, shoulders, ears and mouth. It is closely associated with the functioning of the thyroid gland, which is responsible for the production of hormones that are required for growth, metabolism and maturation.

In the mental framework, the Vishuddha Chakra governs expression – not merely through speech or writing but expression of our inner truth, the purpose of life and the creativity which we utilise to bring that purpose to fruition. This Chakra works as our connection to the spiritual or Akashic realm and relates to our intuitive abilities. The Akashic realm is said to contain the blueprint or perfect template of the other dimensions of the body. This Chakra therefore becomes an important reference point to align the energies of all the Chakras throughout the body.

Physically, the Vishuddha Chakra is depicted as being located just behind the pit of the throat, in the neck region. It is associated with speaking, hence relating it to the mouth, and due to its association with hearing, it is related to the ears as well.

The Vishuddha mandala consists of three main symbols:

- A circle with sixteen petals
- A crescent with a circle inside containing a downward-pointing triangle in which lies another circle

The sixteen petals represent the Siddhis (supernatural powers) that can be acquired through Sadhana and Yoga. The sixteen petals could also be a reference to the sixteen days it takes for the half-moon to develop into the full moon. Here again, it is interesting to note that the Moon is often described as "Nectar Giver" (in keeping with the poison–nectar analogy of this Chakra) in Vedic texts as it nourishes life on earth.

Within the petals lies a silver crescent which is the lunar symbol of nada or pure cosmic sound. The crescent symbolises purity, as purification is a vital aspect of Vishuddha Chakra. The circle can be seen as the development of the crescent into a full moon that represents Akasha.

The animal symbol of the Vishuddha Chakra is a gentle, peace-loving white elephant, the supreme lord of herbivorous animals. In Eastern traditions, a white elephant often carries reference to a royal lifestyle, which promises largesse, riches, prosperity and high status.

The fundamental quality of this Chakra is expression. Expression encompasses our aptitude to hear and speak the truth, internal and external dialogues, and verbal and non-verbal communication. It also comprises our ability to create and project ideas, understand the true purpose or calling of our life and connect with the spiritual realm. It is here that we find our true voice, our highest calling, and we expand it by way of communication and creativity.

To hear and speak the truth is much more difficult than it sounds. Very often we hear what we want to hear, without making an effort to understand what is actually being conveyed. In the same way, we often speak hollow or fake words, giving in to the temptation of saying what the other person wishes to hear. To speak the truth means that we speak with mindfulness and complete awareness, keeping in mind that our personal integrity and authenticity is not compromised. Shellie Crow writes that part of strengthening the Vishuddha Chakra is also about cultivating our voice. "Our voice is more than just the sounds we produce when we want to talk. Our voice is how we outwardly express our inner experiences. We can only borrow the voices of our teachers for so long. Eventually, we must learn to speak in our own voice."

There is a non-stop internal monologue that goes on in our minds at all times. In addition, in modern times we have become accustomed to constantly speak to others (especially on the phone) as a way of connecting with people. We feel a compulsion to engage in talking in order to avoid feelings of boredom or loneliness. In the process, we reduce external dialogues to meaningless banter, which instead of strengthening our sense of communication, further isolates us from the people around us.

Shellie Crow writes that "Good communication is a multi-faceted psycho-spiritual art form that comes from deep and mature self-awareness. One significant aspect of good communication is that there is more than one person involved. Sometimes when we think we are communicating with someone, we are actually just doing a whole lot of talking. It is entirely possible for two parties to engage in a conversation where a whole lot of talking is done but nothing is communicated! One of the most important aspects of good communication is good listening. This is why Vishuddha Chakra governs not only our throat, but our ears as well!

Listening, or attentive reading if one is communicating through signing or writing, is a skill that takes some practice. It is easy to hear what another person says. I can hear the heater kick on. I can hear the sound of my keyboard as I type. However, I'm not really listening to those things. They are just sounds. To listen means that we are tuning out of distractions and tuning into the moment at hand. Listening is a practice of presence."

The Vishuddha Chakra is associated with our sense of sound which we experience through the sense organ of the ears. Sound is carried into the ear by our throat and the vibrations created are felt not just in our body but even in our environment. Udana Vayu, one of the pranas that governs speech, the throat and breath, is active in this Chakra. The Vedas note that the origin of speech occurs in the Manipura Chakra which is the seat of sound, through the energy of fire. It becomes manifest in the throat and is articulated with the help of the tongue and lips where it becomes Vaikhari (the uttered word). The tongue and lips have no control over words as this power lies in the larynx. Paramhans Swami Maheshwarananda says "The ability to be aware of words in their place of genesis – the Manipura Chakra – is very valuable. Words possess a strong power regardless of whether the effect they create is intentional or not. We can seriously harm others and ourselves through words. Therefore, we should speak fewer rather than too many words, and weigh them up in the heart and the Vishuddha Chakra before we speak. A very effective Sadhana for learning control over words is silence (Mauna)."

The Ganapati Atharva Shirsha Upanishad begins with the words "ritam vachmi, satyam vachmi", expressing our desire to speak words that will strengthen both ritam (cosmic truth and order) and satyam (worldly, human truth). It goes on to describe the four degrees of speech, as explained by Vedic expert Robert Svoboda:

- Vaikhari, which is ordinary verbal speech – an expression of kriya shakti, the power of action. You speak in Vaikhari when you focus on deeds past, present activities and exploits to come.
- Madhyama is mental speech, verbalised but unspoken, the internal monologue and dialogue; it expresses jnana shakti, the power of knowledge and wisdom (or lack thereof). Madhyama measures, evaluates, questions and harnesses your rational and emotional minds to formulate the intentions that precipitate into words.
- Pashyanti, single-minded speech, is perceptible but not particularised. It is the vehicle for iccha shakti, the power of desire. When you speak at the pashyanti level, you are sure of your message; your intentions (selfish or altruistic) are always clear.
- Para is pure intention – pure because it is a direct expression of the will of reality, unadulterated by any personal preference. Para is the power of speech that flows directly from the cosmic creatrix. Abhinavagupta, the great genius of a thousand years back, eulogises para as the form of speech that displays absolutely no thought of this, thus, here or now.

The Bija Mantra of the Vishuddha Chakra is "Hum".

The colour associated with this Chakra is a light blue, the most prevalent colour in nature as we perceive the sky to be blue and the vast oceans can range from greenish blue to a bright aqua blue.

An individual with a balanced Vishuddha Chakra experiences a true feeling of harmony between his inner and outer worlds. He is able to express himself freely, articulate his thoughts precisely while exercising full control over his communication. He is patient and mature in his social interactions with a balanced approach towards others. A balanced

Vishuddha Chakra is vital to controlling anger which is almost always an outcome of a lack of communication between the parties concerned. Look back on any situation which made you angry in the past and you will discover that its roots lay either in the fact that you could not make yourself understood, thereby leaving you feeling frustrated or you could not understand the other person's perspective, which made you feel helpless and out of control.

Sundara Krishnaswami writes, "People get angry in many ways. Some explode in momentary rage. Some are slow to anger. Others allow it to fester and nourish the anger in their mind intent on getting even with the person who hurt them. Whether it is a volcanic eruption or a hurt nursed and revenge-plotted anger, it is contra-health and contra-peace." Manu, the Hindu law maker, explains that anger causes eight outcomes: verbal abuse, physical violence, malice, envy, resentment, destruction of valuables, assault and slander.

When the Vishuddha Chakra is out of balance either because of a deficiency or excess, it is manifested as stiffness in the neck and shoulders, frequent sore throat, hoarseness, laryngitis, cancer of the throat, tongue, etc., ear infection, dental issues, and hypo and hyper thyroidism. In the mind, it shows up as shy behaviour, inability to speak clearly, fear of public speaking, loss of voice at crucial times, and on the other end of the spectrum, it leads to overbearing and loud behaviour, brashness and frequent angry outbursts.

You can ask yourself the following questions to check for any imbalance in this Chakra:

- How well do I communicate?
- Do I speak too much or inappropriately often?
- Am I a good listener or do I hear only to prepare a response?
- Do I have a fear of public speaking?
- Can I keep secrets?
- Do I know my vocation and purpose in life?
- Am I taking some action to reach that purpose?
- Am I too shy in social situations?

* Do I often lose my voice?
* Do I tell lies often to boost my self-esteem or in harmless ways?

Here are a few signs that you may be experiencing an imbalance in the Vishuddha Chakra:

* You feel insecure, timid and introverted
* You find it hard to express your emotions in a healthy way
* You often feel misunderstood by others
* You feel anxious during social interactions
* You find yourself in restrictive relationships where you cannot voice your opinion
* You are prone to gossip
* You tend to feel the desire to speak constantly with people just to avoid loneliness
* You are prone to bouts of anger
* You find it difficult to be honest to yourself and others
* You are still seeking your life purpose and often feel that life has no meaning
* You find yourself modifying your reactions to suit other people's needs
* You feel that you are often compared with others
* You suffer from thyroid malfunction
* You have frequent ear or gum infections

Here are some of the best Vishuddha Chakra healing practices:

Learn to really "listen"

We all think we are good listeners when in fact we are just "hearing" most of the time. This is particularly true in the case of close relationships such as a spouse or partner. The closer you are to your partner, the harder you have to work to truly listen to them, says Susan Quilliam, relationship coach and author of *Stop Arguing, Start Talking*. "That security, history and intimacy – being able to finish each other's sentences, treating your partner as if he or she is a part of yourself – can mean our listening gets a little fuzzy. There's a kind of mutual dependency and mental enmeshment that means you really have to struggle hard to listen to your partner as if he or she is a stranger."

You can cultivate the habit of truly listening by doing these things:

- Not talking when others are speaking
- Not formulating a response when you are listening
- Watching for non-verbal clues in the speaker's body language

Choose your words carefully

Words have the ability to literally make or mar a person's life. The power of words is such that a sincere compliment can give great joy while a nasty or angry jibe can do irreversible damage to relationships, careers and personalities. Our minds and bodies carry a cellular memory of cruel words we have uttered as well as endured. It is best if we formulate a sentence in our mind, mull over it for an instant, trying to understand what outcomes it may produce and then go on to actually uttering them. Choosing our words carefully does not mean not being spontaneous or being manipulative in our expression. It just means being conscious of the power of our own speech.

Practice silence

Spending time in silence has long been practiced by Indian yogis as mauna (silence) helps them communicate better with higher levels of consciousness. Silence offers an opportunity for the subtle inner voice to be heard. Robert Svoboda writes, "Overusing, misusing, or abusing any sense organ, your voice in particular, will rob you of the energy you need to speak deeply; try observing silence for an entire day, and you will gain a better understanding of the old maxim 'Speech is energy'. Weakened people can often speak only with their mouths, in Vaikhari; speaking shallowly, they fall easily into shallow breathing, eating, thinking, feeling. Subsisting on life's surfaces, they hustle through existence, hurrying past the silk purse in their pursuit of the sow's ear."

Learn to say "No"

It is in our nature to want to please others, often at a great cost (energy, time, money), which ends up in our saying "yes" when we actually want to say "no". "The ability to communicate 'no' really reflects that you are in the driver's seat of your own life," says Vanessa M. Patrick, "It gives you a sense of empowerment." Saying "no" means learning to be assertive and having a full understanding of what opportunities you actually want to pursue.

Keep a journal

If you have difficulty in verbalising your thoughts, feelings and emotions, you can start to write them down in a private journal. This can be quite cathartic as you are able to express to yourself your deepest, most secret thoughts in the privacy of your space. Making this a daily practice can help in many ways, including overcoming repressed emotions, letting go of all that which no longer serves you and allowing you greater control over self-expression.

Sound healing

Any activity that involves melodious sounds such as singing bowls, gongs, cymbals, playing musical instruments and even singing to yourself is very helpful in balancing this Chakra as these sounds and the vibrations they emit have a profound influence at a cellular level.

Chanting

Studies have shown that chanting of even simple mantras such as "Om" can improve your mood and calm the central nervous system. Chanting is particularly important for this Chakra as it is located in the region of both the tongue and the ears, and therefore, any activity that involves the positive use of sound is highly beneficial in balancing and healing this Chakra. Chanting "Hum" while focusing attention on the throat region and visualising a light blue colour spread smoothly over the area activates the Chakra, removing impurities and balancing the energy.

Food

Healing and soothing food, such as warm water with honey, coconut water, herb tea, soups, are recommended. Blue is not found very often in natural food with the exception of blueberries and blackberries. Seaweeds contain iodine which support thyroid function and have a positive effect on the throat. Chewing consciously and thoroughly are important to ensure proper functioning of the throat Chakra.

Aromatherapy

Aromas have powerful healing properties when used correctly. The throat Chakra responds very well to clean, minty fragrances such as lemon, frankincense, sage, cypress, peppermint, eucalyptus, clove, tree tea and lavender.

Positive affirmations

Affirmations help us to set fresh intentions while letting go and breaking old patterns and habits. To open the throat Chakra, repeat affirmations that relate to authenticity and open communication:

- I communicate confidently and with ease
- I feel comfortable speaking my mind
- I am balanced in speaking and listening
- I am an active listener
- I speak my true thoughts with ease
- I set clear boundaries
- I am in control of my anger
- I think before I speak
- I set clear boundaries

Yoga and Pranayama

Asanas which help in balancing the throat Chakra include:

- Camel pose: Usthrasana
- Plow pose: Halasana
- Cat-Cow pose: Marjarysana
- Shoulder stand: Bhujangasana
- Fish pose: Matsyasana
- Yogic practices such as the Ujjayi (Victorious breath) and Jalandhara Bandha (throat lock) compel the throat to act as a filter, allowing pure oxygen to enter the lungs.

Get a neck massage

The neck and shoulders are regions where we tend to store our stress, and therefore, getting regular neck and shoulder massages help in releasing the lactic acid and energy build up in these regions. Applying a hot pack or a natural muscle relaxant also offer beneficial results in balancing the throat Chakra.

Greeva Basti

An Ayurveda therapy called Greeva Basti, which involves application and retention of warm oil on the back of the neck, is very useful in helping this Chakra heal.

It is in the Visuddha Chakra that we learn that while we cannot change the past, we are certainly creators of our future through the expression of our inner truth. As we begin to articulate and express our emotions and desires in this Chakra, we also learn how to control them. We see how miscommunication is the chief cause of anger and learn the art of anger management by protecting ourselves and others against harsh and impulsive words and actions. We gain a heightened access to different levels of our own consciousness as harmful toxins are removed from the body and negative emotions and feelings are purified in the mental state.

Paramahans Swami Maheshwarananda concludes by stating that "the Vishuddhi Chakra is the gate through which we are able to raise our consciousness to a higher level. It is the border between the physical and astral levels, between consciousness and superconsciousness. When we cross it, the ascent to the realm of wisdom and clarity of consciousness opens up before us." The Vishuddha Chakra not only acts as a cosmic bridge between our heart and mind but also between the spiritual Chakras and our own higher state of being. The Chakra whose chief element is Akasha is a reminder that the Universe is a vast space whose realms we cannot even begin to fathom. The ultimate truth lies in our acknowledgement that we are a part of something immeasurably bigger than our Self. As we tune into our consciousness, we begin to flow with the current of life, discriminating between vidya and avidya (knowledge and ignorance respectively) and feeling a deep sense of joy, completeness and integrity.

11

AJNA CHAKRA
THE EYE OF THE SOUL

"If the single man plant himself indomitably on his instincts, and there abide, the huge world will come round to him."

– Ralph Waldo Emerson

Imagine that you are walking on a sandy, deserted beach on a breezy summer evening. Feel the crunch of the sand under your bare feet. Feel the cool breeze gently fanning your body, making your clothes billow. Think of yourself floating as the waves splash across your feet. Just for a moment, you had created an alternate reality so far removed from your actual present circumstance. What makes this temporary reality possible is the "mind's eye", which enables us to imagine, perceive and think beyond our physical dimension. This is the Third Eye, the Ajna Chakra – the eye that looks inwards instead of outwards.

We all experience the world through our five senses, right from the time we were securely ensconced in our mother's womb where we could touch, taste, hear and even perceive light. As we grow up, we continue to enrich our experiences through our senses and seek more and more stimulation, hoping to expand our awareness. In the Ajna Chakra, we come across our sixth sense – an innate ability to know and intuit without using the faculties of our five senses. We see this sixth sense all around us in nature as animals flee their habitat sensing an upcoming earthquake or flood, or birds knowing exactly when to migrate and when to build nests and lay eggs. At some point before we started depending too heavily on information and data, we, too, had far greater intuitive capacity. We still have this ability; it is just that we have lost faith in it, and an awakening of the Ajna Chakra helps in rebuilding our trust in our own inner guidance system.

The Ajna Chakra is so called because it is the Master Chakra that can control all the other Chakras in the subtle body. "Ajna" in Sanskrit means "to command" or "to call to order". It is here that we transcend the duality of our experiences and realise that the Self is actually not different from and does not exist independently from everything else in the Cosmos. Harish Johari says, "a yogi who has passed through the Vishuddha Chakra at the throat to the Ajna Chakra transcends the five elements and becomes freed (mukta) from the bondage of time-bound consciousness. This is where the I-consciousness is absorbed into super-consciousness."

The Ajna Chakra is represented by a supreme element that is an amalgamation of all the five elements, namely Earth, Water, Fire, Air and Space in their purest forms. It is often seen as symbolising light – offering access to a cosmic vision, dispelling the darkness of our ignorance and illuminating everything without the filter of the past, present or future, and allowing the Third Eye to look beyond the illusion of perceived reality.

In the physical body, this Chakra governs the forehead, base of skull, eyes and lower part of the brain. It is closely associated with the functioning of the hypothalamus, pituitary and pineal glands, which are also considered to be the master glands of the endocrine system. The pineal gland, a tiny pine cone-shaped organ that lies in the centre of the brain, is of particular importance as it regulates the body's circadian clock, determining the body's internal cycles. One of the most important functions is the production of melatonin, the hormone that regulates our sleep-wake cycle, which is crucial for our well-being.

At the mental level, this Chakra helps us connect with our intuition, helping us in making better decisions while allowing us to experience clear thought, spiritual contemplation and reflection. This Chakra is not only the seat of wisdom but also a seat of conscience. It is here that we see and also understand what that "seeing" means. Our sense of fair play, justice and ethics originate here as we determine right from wrong, good from evil and truth from falsehood.

Physically, the Ajna Chakra is between the eyebrows, slightly above the bridge of the nose. Most Western authors depict its location in the centre of the forehead but in the Vedic texts, it is clearly described as lying between the eyes where the eyebrows meet or in the middle of the head behind the eyes.

Hindus believe that spiritual energy from the external environment enters their body through the Ajna Chakra. We see different ways in which they protect this Chakra in the various kinds of spiritual marks such as bindi, application of vermilion, turmeric, sandalwood paste, ash, etc., to ensure that no negative energies can pass through this Chakra.

The mandala of the Ajna Chakra is a transparent lotus with two white petals, said to represent the Ida and Pingala. We have seen the energies of Ida and Pingala separate from the Sushumna channel at the Muladhara Chakra, intertwine their way up through all Chakras and meet again at the Sushumna and become one at Ajna Chakra as it prepares to rise to culminate at the Sahasrara Chakra.

The Maha Kumbh Mela, which sees the biggest congregation of devotees on the planet, takes place once every twelve years in North India. This festival is celebrated at the sacred spot where the physical rivers Ganga and Yamuna (symbolising the Ida and Pingala) meet the mythical river Saraswathi (Sushumna). A specific planetary constellation occurs every twelve years at which time this event is organised. It brings millions of Hindu devotees from across the globe to participate in this massive confluence of spirituality and humanity.

Paramhans Swami Maheshwarananda says, "For a Yogi the true Kumbha Mela occurs in the Ajna Chakra. Ganga, Yamuna and Sarasvati correspond to the main Nadis – Ida, Pingala and Sushumna. The Ajna Chakra, where these three strong energy currents meet in the human body, is also known as Trikuti Tata. In many older illustrations of the Chakras, one can see a twisted white cord made from three threads in the Ajna Chakra. This also symbolises the three Nadis. In India the Brahmins wear such a cord across their chest as a sign of purity of consciousness.

When Yogis purify these three Nadis through concentration, meditation and Pranayama, they are able to keep their consciousness in the Ajna Chakra. With the merging of these three currents of energy in the Sahasrara Chakra, they attain the state of Samadhi, the highest level of consciousness. Just as the Kumbha Mela only takes place every twelve years, it is also only very seldom that all three Nadis are active simultaneously. The body and energy channels are purified by regular practice of Pranayama and Hatha Yoga so that ultimately all three Nadis can be aroused at once with the assistance of concentration and meditation. With this, a radiant light appears in the Trikuti and the Yogis immerse themselves in this light just as the faithful immerse themselves in the holy rivers at the Kumbha Mela. All Karmas are dissolved in this light of divine Love and wisdom."

The two white petals stand for Gu (darkness/ignorance) and Ru (light/knowledge), the two syllables which together form the Sanskrit word "Guru" or Enlightened Master. Inside the pericarp of the lotus a white moon is depicted, within which lies a downward-pointing triangle that contains a Shiva Linga – a symbol of creative consciousness. The same Shiva Linga is seen in the Muladhara Chakra as black in colour while in the Ajna Chakra it is seen having a milky white appearance. This indicates that the consciousness has been purified, with darkness being dispelled by light, as we see in the Peace Mantra:

Asato ma sad gamaya – Lead us from unreality to reality
Tamaso ma jyotir gamaya – Lead us from darkness to light

At this stage, consciousness is not completely pure. It still feels the constant tug in two opposite directions – by the intellect which leads it to retrograde towards the lower Chakras or by sadhana which pushes it towards the highest spiritual Chakra.

The Shiva Linga is an indication of the close link between the Muladhara and Ajna Chakras as these two centres represent the beginning and the end of personal Karma respectively. In the Muladhara Chakra, we started at the level of the unconscious and we have now traversed up the Kundalini to a point where our consciousness is close to becoming one with the Universal Consciousness in the Sahasrara Chakra.

The Ajna Chakra does not have an animal symbol because at this point, we have moved beyond and left behind all our animal instincts.

The fundamental quality of this Chakra is intuition. Everyone experiences a gut feeling at one or more points of time in life. It is different from thinking, reasoning and analysing. It is an unconscious sensation that propels us to act without telling us why or how. There are many examples of how intuition has saved lives and helped mitigate disaster. In 2009 the pilot of an US Airways airplane used his intuition that led to avoiding the imminent death of all passengers aboard a flight that had collided with a flock of birds. Pilots are trained to never use their intuition in a crisis but always follow a logical course of action laid out for them step-by-step. However, the pilot Chesley Sullenberger went against all protocol to land on the Hudson River – a decision that turned out to be a life saver for so many people. Studies have shown that on most occasions, intuition is more efficient than either logic or planning. Yet we choose not to believe in our inner guIdance mechanism because we have been taught throughout our lives to base our decision on reason, hard facts and information. In fact, we are dissuaded from going with our gut feeling on many occasions, landing ourselves in difficult situations, relationships and unnecessary hardships.

Francis P Cholle writes, "Intuition is a process that gives us the ability to know something directly without analytic reasoning, bridging the gap between the conscious and nonconscious parts of our mind, and also between instinct and reason. A gut feeling – or a hunch – is a sensation that appears quickly in consciousness (noticeable enough to be acted on if one chooses to) without us being fully aware of the underlying reasons for its occurrence."

The Ajna Chakra is associated with our sense of sight experienced through the sense organ of our eyes. While our two eyes help us see the physical world, the Third Eye reveals deeper insights. The gift of seeing allows us to experience and internalise the external world. Our eyes are responsible for four-fifths of all the information our brain receives. Vision is a complex process. The brain has to do a lot of work to make a picture. Light passes through the cornea and some of this light enters the eye through an opening called the pupil. The iris (the coloured part of the eye) controls how much light the pupil lets in. Then, light passes through the lens that works together with the cornea to focus light correctly on the retina. When light hits the retina, special cells called photoreceptors turn the light into electrical signals. These electrical signals travel from the retina through the optic nerve to the brain. Then, the brain turns the signals into the images we see.

Everything that we perceive, everything that we experience is a result of the brain interpreting the sensory information that comes in a particular way, says Anil Seth, a neuroscientist. It's just that whenever we agree about what's out there, that's what we call reality. The brain brings to bear its prior expectations about what's out there in order to interpret this massive, noisy and ambiguous sensory information that it continually encounters. Perception is not just a reflection of what we actually see; it is always an active process of interpretation. In fact, we see with our brains. The Ajna Chakra gives us an opportunity to see everything as it really exists from one moment to the next as a mere observer without judgement and without the interference of the brain.

Shiva is always depicted with a "Third Eye" which is seen as a symbol of wisdom and knowledge. When Shiva's Third Eye opens, it burns all that it sees, destroying ignorance and darkness, spreading the light of wisdom and clarity. The Ajna Chakra is the storehouse of knowledge that can help us break the shackles of our Karmas and liberate us so that we can freely continue on our spiritual quest.

The Bija Mantra of the Ajna Chakra is "Aum", the supreme or cosmic sound also known as Pranava. Aum is the sound representation of the ultimate reality – Brahman. It is also called as the Brahmakshara in the *Bhagavada Purana* as it is the root of all mantras and contains all the sounds in the world. Most mantras, prayers and rituals begin and end with Aum; it is the highest of all mantras.

It is the only mantra that has an entire Upanishad (*Mandukya*) devoted to understanding its importance. The Aum is made up of 4 parts; three Devanagari letters – Aah, which is pronounced in the throat with the mouth wide open, Ooh pronounced in the mouth shaped like an O and Mmm which is pronounced by bringing the lips together and creating a pleasant vibration. The fourth part is called "Amatra" or the silence between two mantras.

The three parts of Aum are variously represented as the three states of consciousness – waking, dreaming and sleeping; the three shariras (bodies) – the gross body, the subtle body and the causal body; the three gunas – rajas, sattva and tamas. The fourth part represents the Turiya state – the ever-present consciousness in which the other three states occur.

The verbalisation "Aum" is similar in resonance and frequency as the hum of the Universe. The uttered sound of Aum consists of all the component sounds the human larnyx/mouth is capable of making. Hence, it is seen as a code that can help our consciousness resonate with that of the Universe.

The colour associated with this Chakra is Indigo, often called Royal Blue. Indigo is named after the dye that is obtained from a plant called *Indigofera tinctorial*, commonly found in India where this dye originated from in the ancient times. This deep colour is associated with a sense of deep knowing and innate understanding.

A minor Chakra known as Manas Chakra lies directly above the Ajna Chakra, and it is responsible for sending sense perceptions to the brain. The Manas Chakra lotus is depicted as having six petals, with five representing our five senses and one for sleep. The petals when white take on the colour of the senses which are currently active and are seen to be black during sleep.

An individual with a balanced Ajna Chakra is charismatic, possessing a calm mind, displaying clarity of judgement, strong insight, intuition and emotional balance. When this Chakra is out of balance, it manifests as disharmony between body and mind, aggression, difficulty in focusing, memory loss, nose bleeds, nasal blocks, headache, vision problems, migraine, insomnia and other sleep disorders, seizures and nightmares.

You can ask yourself the following questions to check for any imbalance in this Chakra:

1. Am I having trouble making important decisions?
2. Do I feel disconnected from my intuition?
3. Do I find it difficult to keep an open mind?
4. Was I raised in a close-minded family?
5. Was I encouraged to think freely in my childhood?
6. Did my early life environment offer me emotionally stability?
7. Did my parents value my thoughts and ideas?
8. Do I lack the ability to focus on the task at hand?
9. Do I struggle to see reality clearly and allow my perceptions to colour my judgement?
10. Am I too ready to jump to conclusions?
11. Am I rigid in my thoughts and prejudices?

Here are a few signs that you may be experiencing an imbalance in the Ajna Chakra:

- You tend to be an escapist by going into a state of daydreaming to avoid reality

- You rarely feel creative or inspired by anything
- You do not trust your gut instinct and often overlook your inner guidance
- Your decision making is based on pure logic and data
- You often make inaccurate assessments about people and situations
- Your decisions often turn out to be wrong and lead to losses
- You feel that there is little consonance between your left brain which governs logic and your right brain that is responsible for your creativity
- You have unpleasant dreams and sometimes you have nightmares
- You are not able to recall your dreams easily
- You suffer from frequent eye infections
- You suffer from headaches and migraine very often

Activate Your Pineal Gland

The importance of this small gland lies in the fact that it is now seen as being the "seat of consciousness". The connection between the pineal gland and consciousness can be traced back to Egyptian, Indian and even Tibetan traditions. In Egypt, when the Pharoahs were mummified amidst elaborate processes of embalming and purifying, the pineal gland was removed carefully and placed in a separate jar. The contents of this jar were considered as containing the gateway to the afterlife.

The Tibetans believe that life of an embryo begins on the 49th day after conception. It is interesting to note that it is on the 49th day that the pineal gland starts to develop in a human embryo. This could perhaps explain why the pineal gland is considered the seat of consciousness by experts.

The pineal area is covered in cerebrospinal fluid and has more blood flow per cubic volume than any other organ, making it the gland with the highest concentration of energy in the body. Researchers have found that the pineal gland produces DMT (dimethyltriptamine). DMT is produced when the body goes through extraordinary situations such as extreme physical stress and near-death experiences.

The pineal gland is responsible for the production of melatonin, a hormone that affects the modulation of sleep/wake patterns, which in turn determines the production of other hormones, controls stress levels and regulates seasonal circadian rhythms in the body. Melatonin is known to have anti-aging and anti-stress properties; it is involved in the suppression of cortisol while working as a powerful antioxidant.

The pineal gland is not protected by the blood–brain barrier, and therefore, cannot defend itself against harmful toxins that enter the bloodstream. Specific toxins, such as synthetic fluoride and chloride, are shown to have an affinity for the pineal gland, weakening its abilities to produce neurotransmitters and receive photons of light from external sources.

It is important, therefore, to ensure that the pineal gland is working at its optimal in order to enjoy the benefits of spiritual growth and awareness.

Our bodies are made up of almost 75% of water. It is very important to consume adequate amounts of water to ensure activation of the pineal gland. Additionally, a balanced diet that is high in tryptophan is helpful in providing the building blocks for the important biochemical produced by the pineal gland. Tryptophan is found in many food, including eggs, most kinds of seeds (including sesame, chia, sunflower, pumpkin), most nuts (maximum content in almonds, pistachios, hazelnuts), dark chocolate and bananas.

Indians follow the tradition of sun worship since Vedic times. Exposure to early morning sun stimulates the pineal gland. Exposure to sunlight is necessary for other body functions as well, and it is recommended that you spend at least 10 to 15 minutes of the day under the sun, preferably in the early morning, to enjoy optimal health and well-being.

It is also important to spend time in total darkness as this helps the pineal gland to suppress serotonin and increase melatonin, which is necessary to induce sleep. A dark environment in the bedroom is very important to ensure a good night's rest.

You should especially avoid blue light which comes from sources such as the television, computer screens and smart phones. Blue light can lead to a stimulation of serotonin as the body thinks it is daytime, therefore upsetting the wake and sleep cycle.

Gently tapping your forehead in between your eyebrows activates the pineal gland. The vibration sends a wave directly back to the pineal gland, activating it in the process.

Pressing your tongue against the roof of your mouth activates the pituitary gland and through its physical and chemical connections, activates the pineal gland and hypothalamus as well. This method is also used in Ayurveda and Yoga, and is akin to the kechari mudra practised by ancient seers.

It is a well-known fact that our energy flows to wherever our attention goes. Focusing our attention on the pineal gland will help activate it. Visualisation cannot take place without the use of the Third Eye. You can choose to practice any form of visualisation or guided imagery to help the pineal gland become more active.

Meditation has numerous benefits that are often written about. But one of the lesser-known benefits of mindfulness is better activation of the pineal gland. Meditating guides bio-electric energy to the pineal gland, thereby facilitating a greater sense of clarity and also improves intuition.

Chanting causes the tetrahedron bone in the nose to resonate, which creates a stimulation of the pineal gland. Chanting Aum has special resonance with the Ajna Chakra.

The physical benefits of an active pineal gland can be felt in various aspects of living such as finding a greater balance in our work–life ratio, improved well-being, better functioning of bio-rhythms and improved hormonal states. In terms of emotional benefits, you will find that you are calmer, better at decision making, more at peace with yourself and others, and you find a renewed zest for living.

Increase Self-Awareness

Open yourself up to new thoughts and ideas, and learn from the wisdom of others through reading, listening or following. You can also dive into your own insight to look at things from a new perspective.

Build your intuition

Practice building up your intuition by setting yourself small intentions and then pay attention to find ways of fulfilling them. Start with simple intentions and as you begin to build trust in your own insight, make your goals bigger and bigger while looking out for the intuitive signals.

Pay close attention to your dreams

The purpose of dreams and their connection to our subconscious and conscious minds fascinated Sigmund Freud who wrote his seminal work *The Interpretation of Dreams* in 1899. To this day, the subject is highly researched by neuroscientists and psychologists. Mihaela Bernard writes that there are five reasons why we should pay attention to our dreams:

- Dreams provide us with insight about our deepest thoughts and feelings.
- They help us make sense of our daily experiences and enable us to remember.
- They allow us to think and feel things our conscious mind may not want to think or feel.
- They speak in images and symbols that need to be deciphered.
- They can lead us to a better understanding of ourselves and our relationship to others.

Many people claim they do not dream at all, but studies have shown that every person spends a substantial quantity of their REM sleep time in a dream state. It may just be that such people do not remember their dreams. Dream journaling is particularly useful for them.

Practice Trataka

Trataka is an ancient Ayurvedic practice that has been used for millennia by yogis and is based on the idea that our eyes are the pathway to the mind and the soul. This simple, yet powerful, practice involves gazing fixedly on an object or a candle flame without blinking. When our attention is focused on an object, our thoughts are focused and the mind goes into a steady state. Our thoughts get less and less turbulent and slowly the mind comes under control. Trataka should not be practiced for more than 10 minutes at a time and it is best done initially under the guidance of a qualified teacher. Regular practice is said to bring about improved cognitive functioning, balance activities of the two spheres of the brain and soothe cranial nerves, while improving vision.

Caution

This exercise is not suitable for people with mental health issues. Those who suffer from depression, anxiety, etc., should not practice Trataka. Also, do not practice trataka on a candle if you have cataract, glaucoma, myopia, astigmatism or epilepsy.

Food

Eat food that is dark in colour such as dates, blackberries, figs, raisins, eggplant and purple cabbage. These are very good for activation of this Chakra.

Aromatherapy

Use fragrances such as patchouli, sandalwood, vetiver, juniper and clarysage.

Yoga

Asanas beneficial for the Ajna Chakra include postures which allow the forehead to touch the ground such as

- Child pose: Balasana
- Forward bend pose: Uttanasana
- Head to knee pose: Janushirshasana
- Dolphin pose: Ardha Pincha Mayurasana
- Yoga mudra

Shirodhara

An Ayurveda therapy called Shirodhara, which involves the slow dripping of warm oil on the forehead, is very useful in helping this Chakra heal.

Affirmations

* I am in touch with my inner guidance
* I trust my intuition
* I seek to understand and to learn from my life experiences.
* I nurture my spirit
* It is safe for me to see the truth
* I forgive the past and learn what was there for me to learn
* I am connected with the wisdom of the Universe
* I am open to inspiration and bliss
* My life moves effortlessly
* I am at peace
* I am the source of my truth and my love
* My thoughts are calm and peaceful
* I see with clarity

With a balanced and harmonious Ajna Chakra, your intuition becomes your constant guide that you come to trust fully. Both hemispheres of the brain work in synchrony, balancing your creativity with your logical ability. You begin to examine the deeply entrenched ideas that are possibly obstructing your growth, and begin to develop a wisdom that transcends the duality of life. You begin to actually "see" the truth in each situation and person. Intuition will help you make decisions that will allow you to fulfil and manifest your deepest desires. Life will suddenly take on more easy, fluid and positive attributes as the development of our wisdom is almost complete at this point. We have now truly been led from darkness to light, from ignorance to knowledge and from attachment to liberation.

As the Ajna Chakra blossoms, we become more attuned to our own clairvoyance and begin to see with greater clarity within ourselves and the world outside. As Paramhans Swami Maheshwarananda says, "The gifts of clairvoyance, intuition and telepathy lie in the Ajna Chakra. When we strengthen the power of concentration and learn to perceive all the energy assembled in the Ajna Chakra, our mind can receive or transmit knowledge through time and space. The function of the Ajna Chakra is comparable to a searchlight, which can, through the concentration of light, make things visible at a distance. Those whose Ajna Chakra is opened are at home in all three worlds – past, present and future."

12

SAHASRARA CHAKRA
SEEK AND YOU WILL FIND

"In my soul there is a temple, a shrine, a mosque, a church where I kneel."

– Rabia al-Basri

We have now reached the seventh and highest Chakra which acts as our connection with the Divine and reveals to us our own inherent spiritual nature. The word "Sahasrara" refers to the thousand-petalled lotus that is symbolic of this Chakra. "Sahasra" in Sanskrit means "a thousand" and often implies an infinite number. This Chakra, also known as the Crown Chakra, allows us to directly experience an intimate relationship with the Cosmos, while giving us a glimpse of the eternal. Many scholars argue that the Sahasrara is not technically a Chakra but merely a powerful energy centre which is both giver and recipient of our consciousness. In our bodies, it is here that we find the seat of cosmic consciousness which is also present in everything in the Universe.

The Sahasrara Chakra is depicted as being located on the crown of the head beneath the fontanelle, which is easily visible in a new-born child, and the energy is palpable up to about two inches above the head. We often see images of a halo that surrounds holy men. It is located just above the body – this is the aura of the Crown Chakra. One of the reasons why we see religious people in India always keeping their head covered with some sort of headgear is to protect this divine and potent energy centre from negative external influences. It is at the Sahasrara that the Sushumna Nadi terminates as consciousness and becomes one with the Universe. The Sahasrara Chakra is the location where the Kundalini Shakti, having risen from the depths of the Muladhara, now unites with Shiva. This union occurs when the stream of energy from the Ida and Pingala unite and rise through the Sushumna Nadi. It is for this reason that the Sahasrara is seen as containing the purest form of prana.

Katie Ness writes, "The Crown Chakra is our warehouse for energies we amass through kind thoughts and actions and through acts of faith, meditation and prayer. It is where we can transcend dimensions of life and commune with God."

In connection with the physical body, the Crown Chakra is the entry point for the human life-force, which pours abundantly into the body's energy system from the greater Universe. It is this force that nourishes the body, mind and spirit, and energy is distributed throughout the physical body all the way down to the lower Chakras. At the time when the Kundalini ascends to the Sahasrara Chakra, the spiritual practitioner experiences a dissolution of his sense of self as he becomes one with the Universe. This state is called samadhi – a state in which there is no activity in the mind as the distinction between knower and knowledge becomes blurred and the mind finds repose in sat-chit-ananda or the Ultimate Bliss.

The Sahasrara Chakra is represented by what can only be termed as the "causal space" – the seed from which all things manifest. While the Ajna Chakra acts as the gateway to this space where all the five elements came together as a supreme element, all the other lower Chakras also act like rungs of a ladder, allowing the ascendance of the energy. It is often said that while the other six Chakras are only switches, the actual potential only lies in the Sahasrara.

Paramhans Swami Maheshwarananda says, "The element of the Sahasrara Chakra is Adi Tattva. It is the source of creation, the pure light and one reality. This Tattva is Adi Anadi. 'Adi' means 'without beginning', 'Anadi' means 'without end' – therefore infinite. As soon as this Tattva unites with a quality (guna), it is bound and therefore limited – just as pure water has no taste of its own, but is modified by and takes on the taste of whatever is added to it. In the Cosmos there are diverse manifestations of this one Tattva with various qualities and functions – such as fire, water, air and earth – but the basis is always the same, the pure essence."

In the physical body, this Chakra governs the brain, central nervous system and the cerebral cortex. It also has an impact on the working of the pituitary gland, pineal gland and the hypothalamus.

At the mental level, it allows us to access our inner wisdom, generate devotion, feel connected to others, gain inspirational or prophetic insights, see the bigger picture and feel a sense of calm and wholeness regardless of the situation we are facing.

The mandala of the Sahasrara Chakra is a lotus with a thousand petals made up of different colours. The petals are arranged in 20 layers with 50 petals each. The pericarp is golden and within it lies a circular moon which contains a triangle which can either be upward or downward pointing.

The fundamental quality of this Chakra is detachment. "Detachment is not that you should own nothing, but that nothing should own you."

We all are guilty of attachment to people, the work that we do, our possessions, our habits, beliefs and prejudices. We find it unimaginable to let go of this tie-up, feeling that if we lose the person, thing or habit we are attached to, we will somehow become incomplete and lose our own carefully crafted definition of ourselves. Attachment, therefore, becomes anything that defines us in some way – the work that we do, the house and cars that we own, the people that we relate to, the situations that mould our personalities, the habits that drive us. We begin to associate with them so closely that we think we have become that. A CEO, a mother, a PhD holder, a smoker – we start to see ourselves as one or all of these things. We do not stop to think that we will still remain the same if we lose all these aspects of life. When we start to recognise that our real self is not in any way deficient because of our lack of these external aspects is when true detachment can begin to set in.

Osho says, "Remain in the world, act in the world, do whatsoever is needful and yet remain transcendental, aloof, detached, a lotus flower in the pond." This is the precise lesson of the Sahasrara Chakra.

The term "Vairagya" is used frequently in Hindu philosophy. It is found in Patanjali's Yoga Sutras where it is called the key to restrain the mind along with Abhyasa, which refers to a disciplined practice. It is a Sanskrit word which roughly translates to detachment and renunciation.

There are three degrees of Vairagya, as explained in our ancient texts:

1. Mridhu or mild
2. Madhyama or moderate
3. Teevra or intense

Our texts discuss that there are two occasions when Vairagya is felt most profoundly – one upon the death of a loved one called Smashana Vairagya ("Smashana" means "crematorium or graveyard") and the other felt by a mother after just having given birth to a child known as Prasuti Vairagya. When we lose a person whom we have loved dearly, the grief is such that we begin to see the futility of all our pursuits, wondering why we struggle so much to achieve our ends when ultimately, we will also end up just like our loved one. The mother, after having gone through the extreme pain of child birth, thinks to herself that she will never go through this experience again and introspects about the entire nine months of struggle she has gone through to give birth. In both instances, time is a great healer and as the pain subsides, we go back to our normal course of living, forgetting all about the momentary detachment we had experienced.

Markata Vairagya or monkey dispassion is often quoted as an example of an apparent disinterest in life which may arise because of ulterior motives, especially in so-called spiritual gurus or self-proclaimed Godmen. Jagadguru Srila Bhakti Siddhant Saraswati Goswami Thakur Prabhupad says,

"To a superficial eye, monkeys are engaged in renunciation because they live naked in the forest without any fixed home. In fact, they are only interested in their own sensual enjoyment and have never given it up. Such show-bottle renunciation is called markata – vairagya, 'monkey-renunciation.'"

Vairagya has four stages:

1. Yatamana – efforts to lead the mind away from seeking sensual pleasures
2. Vyatireka – a "logical discontinuance" as one becomes aware of one's dispassion towards objects
3. Ekendriya – the senses remain subdued with the mind having attachment or aversion to an object
4. Vasirara – there exists no temptation, there are no likes or dislikes

Vairagya cannot be gained by making changes to our external lifestyle. It is an internal state of mind that needs to be cultivated by applying "viveka" or discrimination to all our life experiences. Vairagya is not just about suppressing our desires and distancing ourselves from material objects. It is Teevra Vairagya alone that can make self-realisation possible. Paramhans Swami Maheshwarananda aptly describes it thus:

"To free ourselves from attachments does not mean to walk away from our family or neglect our duties. It is much more about the inner removal of the fear of separation, jealousy and the desire for possessions and power. To free ourselves from these ties is allied with mental discipline and work. It is hard for us to motivate ourselves, to do without something, to give up something or to forgive someone. Remove the chains of attachment! Only our ignorance keeps us trapped in dependency, sorrow and pain. It causes all the problems. Give love without attachment, because real love gives freedom!

Vairagya (renunciation) is a prerequisite for the attainment of true knowledge. To attain the eternal we must let go of the transitory. Vairagya is an inner occurrence – the extinction of our wishes and desires. These always produce new Karma, and when they 'dry up', the river of Karma runs dry by itself."

The *Bhagavad Gita* explains that after our worldly journey comes to an end, we move into an astral plane appropriate to our Karma. In this plane, we remain utterly aware of everything that is going on around us but do not have the ability to act as we lack a vehicle, such as our body, to participate in the event. There are three possibilities that arise: a soul with some leftover negative Karma takes a new birth in some animal form, one with better Karmas takes on a human form while the soul who has exhausted its Karma, attains moksha by becoming one with the Universal Consciousness.

When death occurs, the soul is seen as leaving the physical body through one of the nine orifices – mouth, eyes, nostrils, excretory organs or genitals. It is only the soul of a liberated yogi that departs from the Sahasrara Chakra. There are many documented cases of Indian yogis such as Paramahamsa Yogananda who left their earthly bodies in this manner through the process of Mahasamadhi.

The Sahasrara Chakra is not associated with any special colour or quality. Its light contains all colour vibrations united in the incomparable brilliance of pure light. Says Paramhans Swami Maheshwarananda, "No other light approaches the brilliance of the sun. In the same way, the radiance of all the other Chakras fades before the incomparable radiance of the Sahasrara Chakra."

A minor Chakra known as the Bindu Chakra lies close to the Sahasrara Chakra, at the back of the head where Brahmins retain a tuft of hair. The symbol of this Chakra, which is also sometimes referred to as the Soma Chakra, is a crescent moon with a bindu placed just over it. This Chakra is seen as the exact point through which the soul enters the body, creating the Chakras as its energy spirals downwards and terminates in the Kundalini at the Muladhara Chakra.

An individual with a balanced Sahasrara Chakra is seen having an open and balanced mind, connected with himself and others, showing empathy and non-judgemental acceptance of everything around him. He shows signs of a keen passion for life, often experiencing a sense of flow and transcendence in the course of pursuing his work or passion. An imbalance, on the other hand, shows up as a lack of connectedness with self and others, a deep sense of aloneness and an inability to relate to matters of the spirit. It can also manifest as a dogmatic, rigid approach to religion with a narrow-minded vision, unable to grasp the bigger picture, prone to attributing their problems to others and carrying along with them a skewed perception of all aspects of life. It also shows up as mental disorders like schizophrenia, neuralgia, Parkinson's and Alzheimer's.

You can ask yourself the following questions to check for any imbalance in this Chakra:

1. Do I feel a balanced connection with my own spiritual nature?
2. Does my work take on a spiritual meaning or is it just a means of earning a livelihood?
3. Do I find myself undertaking some humanitarian efforts from time to time?
4. Do I often feel frustrated about where I am in life currently?
5. Do I feel joy in the small things of life?
6. Do I have any destructive feelings towards myself or others?
7. Do I find myself overly addicted to spiritual endeavours?
8. Do I neglect my duties in search of spiritual experiences?
9. Do I feel a sense of loneliness?
10. Do I feel a lack of empathy for others?

Here are a few signs that you may be experiencing an imbalance in the Sahasrara Chakra:

* You choose to lead a very stressful, fast-paced life
* You have unresolved trauma from your childhood or early years
* You feel too much attachment to people, objects and situations
* You feel alienated from the world around you
* You feel like the Universe is not supportive of your endeavours
* You feel unlucky
* You feel a lack of purpose and sense of direction
* Small things make you question your own faith in living
* You often find yourself bored and vacant
* You suffer from chronic fatigue
* You enrol for retreats, yoga lessons, meditation courses once too often
* You suffer from headaches
* You have nightmares frequently
* You are often delusional

Here are some of the best Sahasrara Chakra healing practices:

Commit Yourself to a Spiritual Practice

Advaita Vedanta clearly indicates that self-realisation can only be achieved through an intense spiritual practice. Sadhana is a Sanskrit term which means "spiritual exercise employed to achieve a specific goal". Sadhana can involve meditation, prayer, physical austerities, chanting, fasting or ritual worship. The key here is consistency and discipline regardless of the type of practice. Sri Adi Shankaracharya describes the four-fold path called Sadhana Chatushtaya in Vivekachudamani, as consisting of:

* Viveka (discrimination)
* Vairagya (detachment)

- Shatsampatti (the six virtues which we have discussed earlier)
- Mumukshutva (a burning desire to attain a goal)

This path allows the mind to become calm as the practitioner begins to rely more on the Vignanamaya Kosha (the intellectual sheath), moving away from the impulsive drives that arise from a dependence on the Manomaya Kosha (the mental sheath).

Sadhguru defines Sadhana thus:

"Everything can be sadhana. The way you eat, the way you sit, the way you stand, the way you breathe, the way you conduct your body, mind and your energies and emotions – this is sadhana. Sadhana does not mean any specific kind of activity, sadhana means you are using everything as a tool for your well-being."

Practice Detachment

Detachment is not easy and takes a great deal of time, effort and energy, sometimes much more than it took to form the attachment. The first step therefore is to avoid attachment as much as possible. It is best to start with small steps such as letting go at first of your feelings and emotions. Watch your mind as an outsider and see why you feel a certain way about something. Then, allow the feeling to let go as if you are letting go of a balloon you are holding on to for too long. Practising being in the moment also helps in bringing about a sense of detachment, especially from past memories and situations. Make an effort to move forward every single day from your present situation, even if it is just one small step at a time.

Simplify Your Life

Decluttering your life is a two-step process. First, you identify what is important to you and the second is to get rid of everything else. Evaluate your commitments in every aspect of life – relationships, work, love, material possessions and even the memories that you carry. Make extensive lists if required as these will help you understand and prioritise better. People who no longer serve you or bring in a negative energy must be the first thing you address as they are the prime reason for day-to-day stress. Then, move on to identifying all aspects of your life which need simplification and take on each one as a dedicated project. Ask yourself before each major decision: Will this simplify my life? If the answer is no, then sleep over it.

Find a Guru

Having a teacher to guide us in any field is invaluable. In spirituality, we are dealing with subjects that are esoteric, subtle and intangible. The concepts are often difficult to grasp, the language of the Scriptures are not known to us, and above all, we may not have had the necessary exposure to the basic tenets of the practice, which makes it imperative for us to have someone to turn to when a question or problem arises in the course of our studies.

Zamir Dhanji writes that "in Sanskrit, 'Guru' refers to a spiritual teacher who leads a willing student to the realisation of their true nature. There are numerous stories from spiritual lore of the fated encounters between Guru and Disciple – many aspirants on the spiritual path hunger to one day meet their guru. But the journey it takes to prepare us to recognise and follow an authentic Guru cannot be planned. We must walk the journey for it to become our own."

A guru's grace and blessings are absolutely essential to progress on the spiritual path.

Meditate on the Sri Chakra Yantra

The Sri Chakra Yantra is a magical tool that stimulates and concentrates the psychic forces that you engage in. In Tantra, creation and destruction are seen as a continuum and all manifestations – from the grossest to the subtlest – are eventually connected and are one and the same.

(For more information on the Sri Chakra Yantra, you can read my book by the same name published by Notion Press)

In case you do not possess a copper Sri Chakra, you use an accurate black and white representation printed on paper rather than a coloured one as colours tend to have inherent associations which we wish to avoid at this stage. I would suggest that you do not use an image on the laptop, computer screen, TV screen or mobile screen as the energy emitted by electronic devices may interfere with the energy fields.

The most ideal location is a small area dedicated to your practice. This will help you gain focus faster as your practice progresses. Choose a place to sit, preferably on the floor with a mat. You must be facing east, sitting in the north-east quadrant of your space. The Sri Chakra Yantra should be placed directly before you in the east direction at a distance of about one foot from you at eye level. You must be able to clearly discern the different lines and patterns without straining the eyes.

Begin by folding your hands in prayer and chanting Om three times to bring your mind into focus.

Focus on your breath and notice how it slows down when you observe it consciously. Allow your entire body to relax as you breathe normally, but with awareness. Keep your face relaxed at all times by smiling very gently and effortlessly.

Slowly take your eyes to the bindu and let it rest there gently. Do not stare or fix your gaze tightly. Without moving your eyes, gradually take in the triangle that contains the bindu and take in the beauty of the symmetrical design. Allow your vision to expand to the next set of triangles and rest your focus on each set for as long as you are comfortable doing so. Then, bring the first set of petals into focus and feel your gaze extending outward just as the petals are seen blossoming. Include the second set of petals in your line of vision and let your attention grasp the entire pattern for a while.

Now slowly recognise the three concentric circles and allow them to enter you line of vision. Slowly acknowledge the square with the four gateways and let your eyes gaze upon the entire pattern in unity. Keep your focus there for as long as you can while continuing to breathe slowly and calmly, feeling a deep sense of relaxation taking over your mind and body.

Now slowly bring your attention from the square to the circles as you proceed on an inward journey through the various shapes in the Sri Yantra. Arrive at the triangle that encloses the bindu and focus your attention there briefly before making the bindu your sole focus of attention. At this time, your gaze should almost be bringing your attention to the area between your eyebrows. Rest your gaze there as you have arrived at the point of cosmic dissolution from where creation begins again.

Slowly close your eyes and bring your attention from the bindu to your breath and keep your eyes closed as you try to visualise the yantra in your mind's eye. Sit in the same meditative position for a few minutes before gently getting up after folding your hands in the prayer position. Do not be tempted to judge your experience or be disappointed if you feel no different from before you took up the meditation.

Understand that the exercise you have undertaken is making changes in your brain and will continue to do so for as long as you remain steadfast in your practice. This change in brain structure is scientifically known as neuroplasticity, and meditation has been one of the most well-accepted methods to change patterns in the brain.

As you expand your vision from the bindu to the square, you are participating in a meditative method that involves evolution (extending outward from the centre to multiply into an array of creativity). Evolution symbolises our gradual moving from the Divine to all the aspects of the outer world while understanding that the subtle worlds give rise to the mundane and the gross.

As you bring your attention back from the square to the bindu, you are involved in a method that is known as involution (collapsing inward from the perimeter to the centre). Involution is the moving away from the gross and dualities towards the subtle and non-dualistic reality. You dissolve all misconceptions to become one with the Divine.

Meditate

Meditation is a wonderful way of centring the body, mind and soul, and contrary to popular belief, it is very simple and easy to do. Meditation leaves you feeling calmer, balanced, creative and healthy. You can start meditating by merely focusing on your breath and noting the thoughts that flit past your mind.

The idea behind meditation is not to have a completely blank mind but to clear the mind of thoughts for that time alone. Just watching your thoughts, not zeroing in on one thought and letting go of the thought once it has arisen in the mind is one of the ways of meditating.

You can also use a mantra or an affirmation to bring yourself into a meditative frame of mind. It is also very important to meditate on the thought of death each day. This will help you over come your fear of death as you slowly come to the understanding that if death comes, you will merely be shedding this mortal body.

Choose Your Sensory Inputs

Our surroundings are constantly bombarding us with negativity. Newspapers and television channels highlight all the things that are wrong with the world and the message we send to our minds is that nothing is right, lawful or fair anymore. This is far from the truth. We are actually living in the best of times, with fewer wars and lesser number of poor people than ever before in history. Be judicious in your choice of reading newspapers and books, watching television programmes, browsing the internet and in interactions with people. Avoid news items and films with violence, and seek content, such as meaningful documentaries and stories, that nourish the soul.

Yoga

- Headstand: Sirsasana
- Rabbit Pose: Sasangasana
- Corpse Pose: Savasana
- Half Lotus Pose: Ardha Padmasana
- Tree Pose: Vrishshasana
- Plow pose: Halasana
- Seated Forward Bend: Paschimottanasana
- Supported Headstand: Salamba Sirsasana
- Alternate Nostril Breathing: Nadi Shodhana Pranayama

Shirobasti

A complex Ayurvedic treatment known as Shirobasti, which involves shaving off the hair and then applying medicated oils, is said to bring extensive benefits to the head region.

Affirmations

- I am connected to the Universe.
- I am at peace
- I see the Divine in everyone
- I have clear spiritual insight
- I am open to the abundance of the Universe
- I am capable of manifesting my desires
- I accept myself totally
- I am whole and complete
- I honour my body, mind and spirit
- I am open to the wisdom of the Universe
- I am healed at all levels of my being
- I let go of my attachments
- I live in the present moment
- I am utterly grateful for everything

Preserve Medha Shakti

The brain constantly supplies us with the necessary energy to harness our mental capacities, to make and retain memories, and to ensure optimal coordination amongst all parts of the body. This energy is known as Medha Shakti in Ayurveda, and it is necessary to take steps to preserve and strengthen this important energy source, especially in current times when cognitive diseases such as Alzheimer's and dementia appear to be steadily on the rise amongst all cultures across the world. Medha Shakti can be strengthened by practising deep relaxation methods such as meditation, pranayama, yoga and also by consuming nutritious, sattvic food with high prana such as fresh, locally grown fruits and vegetables, almonds, walnuts and the like. It is also imperative to keep the brain active by engaging it in challenging activities such as learning a new language or musical instrument, solving puzzles or memorising mantras.

The Muladhara Chakra grounded us to earth; the Sahasrara tethers us to the spirit. We have reached the final milestone of our journey through the Chakras and arrived at the much-awaited destination. Our ancient texts describe the Sahasrara Chakra as the seat of our soul which provides us with the only known way to attain enlightenment. An energised Sahasrara Chakra may not offer us a transcendent experience but it certainly can help us become calmer, gain greater clarity of vision, and feel a sense of belonging and understand the interconnectedness of everything in the Cosmos. Our lives become rejuvenated and revived as we are overcome with gratitude at the serenity and sense of expansiveness that now defines our reality.

The development of our consciousness is a comprehensive process that rarely occurs instantaneously. Using the allegory of the lotus, our progress is similar to that of a seed which embeds itself in the soil for some time before it springs up as a tiny sprout longing for life and then continues to grow both upwards and downwards as the plant reaches out of the water with its branches and leaves while the roots make their way into the earth. Our first step towards consciousness is taken in the Muladhara Chakra as we move upward till we reach the thousand-petalled brilliance of the Sahasrara Chakra.

Every individual's journey is a different one, made up of our own experiences – good and bad – and charting a unique course which no other person can fully fathom or comprehend. While our paths are different, our destination is fixed and final. We have no say in this matter. The paths we choose bring pleasure and pain, sickness and good health, love and apathy, struggles and successes, but the eventual outcome depends entirely on how purposefully we have followed our spiritual quest. Have we lived true to our purpose with self-discipline and willpower? Have we sacrificed the temporal, fleeting pleasures for a more abiding peace? Have we understood that our true happiness lies entirely within us and is unrelated to our external circumstances? If we can safely answer these questions with a yes, then the development of our consciousness is possibly complete and we no longer stare at the bleak prospect of endless cycles of birth and rebirth as we are sure to be enveloped in the nothingness of moksha as we become one with the Universal Consciousness.

13
CONCLUSION

"The human body, most precisely the Chakras – the vortices of consciousness in the body – are the gateway to discovering the mystery of the Universe and our life in it."

– Pandit Rajmani Tigunait

The Chakras offer deep insights into our physiological, psychological and spiritual state while serving as a route map to understand the meaning and purpose of our life as individuals. From a collective perspective, we see that the world that we live in is also trying to cope with several imbalances at every Chakra level:

Muladhara

Research suggests that since the 1950s, humans have become more and more distanced from nature and its life-giving benefits. One of the biggest reasons is the trend of urbanisation which destroys nature and removes people from natural surroundings. Technological changes, such as the advent of the television and more recently, the Internet, have more or less substituted nature as a source of recreation and entertainment. We, as a species, feel deeply disconnected from Mother Earth and continue to exploit her largesse and generosity.

Swadisthana

If the times we live in can be described in three words, it would be money, sex and power. The desire to accumulate wealth has become the overriding aim of almost every person on the planet. Sex is no longer a sacred act of union between two loving individuals. It is now a mere commodity – used as a means to sell everything from soap to cars. Sex brings in big money as porn proliferates and debases sex even more, creating addicts and fuelling perversions. And power – that's the one thing that people lust after even more than money and sex as it promises more of both when achieved.

Manipura

We live in a world with unlimited and easy access to information and know more than ever before. This is also the same world that is filled with misinformation, designed carefully to manipulate our thoughts. Elections are won, products are sold, celebrities are made this way. Most of what we consume though is bad news or negative in nature as stories of goodness, morality and humanity get buried deep underneath the desire for the morbid, violent and sensational. We have all got used to consuming mindless information about celebrity lifestyles, following their every move on social media. The media is conveniently blamed for misinformation while we turn a blind eye to the fact that the media only supplies what people demand.

Anahata

Our dependence on technology has alienated us from our fellow human beings. We meet future partners online more often than in real life. The personalities we create for ourselves on social media are often so far removed from who we really are that we give out wrong messages, leading to failure in relationships. When this happens once too often, we lose faith in the institution of love and romance. Human connections, friendship and love are all crucial to the well-being of individuals and societies and when these important threads that form the fabric of the world are weakened, it leads to collective fear, distrust and a deep-seated sadness.

Vishuddha

We have allowed our lives to be entirely governed by social media and the bunch of lies it perpetrates. Communication today is all about either being polite or being politically correct, never about being true to ourselves. If we dare to express our opinion, which may not be mainstream, we are trolled until we exit the scene. The anonymity that social media guarantees has actually brought out the ugliest side of humanity, with its meanest heads rearing in the comments section of all platforms. We are literally roaming like souls lost in the realm of the internet space with no recourse to the grounding energies of Earth or Water.

Ajna

Save for a small percentage of the world population who is keen on exploring their spiritual side, the rest of the world continues to live in a state of animal consciousness, seeking only to fulfil the needs of their baser instincts. Society, in general, is not very encouraging to the seekers as it is threatened by the fear that such seekers may eventually choose to remain outside the periphery of social controls. The Maharishi Effect is a well-known phenomenon which has shown that even a small percentage of population practising some form of spirituality has a big, positive impact on society at large. A group of meditators in a small town can actually help bring down crime levels and instances of suicide in their circle. Yet, there is no incentive offered to those who wish to pursue the spiritual path. Those who do so in spite of all the resistance they face, know that the outcome is incentive enough.

Sahasrara

We are seeing major world religions thrust their beliefs on others, global leaders who support bigotry and racism, clerics support terrorist activities in the name of punishing the "unfaithful", promising martyrdom to the perpetrators of such heinous acts as bombings and mass killings. Such events create a huge sense of fear and mistrust among populations, which permeates generations to come. Most people start feeling a sense of disconnectedness with the Universe when they have to constantly face situations of uncertainty and loss. The state of our external world is the single biggest cause for the unprecedented angst and sense of meaninglessness that the world is experiencing today.

Even the most basic aspects of our perception are shaped and sharply influenced by our surroundings and our cultural orientation. Over time, these cultural influences become deeply ingrained in our psyche and affect our overall sense of well-being. It is obvious that living in such skewed social circumstances is bound to have an impact on us as individuals and lead to an imbalance in the Chakras. As we gain greater awareness and insight of not just the internal world of our Chakras but also of the external world that we live in, we carry in ourselves the potential to grow not merely as individuals but also collectively as a society. As more and more people establish their own inner balance, society will slowly find itself becoming more stable and more spiritually awakened.

The Vedic text *Chakravidya* speaks of the relationship between stages of human development and the seven Chakras. In the first seven years of our life, we are influenced by the Muladhara Chakra, which is related to security, stability and family ties. In these first years of life, all experiences are about understanding the world around us as we learn to identify whom we can trust, how we can communicate using language, learn more about the planet and its working, and start to seek more information about the Universe. Ages 7-14 is dominated by the Swadisthana Chakra which has to do with finding our creativity and coming to terms with our sexuality. It is in these years that a child develops into a teen, gaining an understanding of sexuality from its maturing body. It is during this time that we figure out who we want to be and what we want to do as individuals. The Manipura Chakra, which represents our sense of self, rules over the ages of 15-22 years as we become individuals in our own right, developing our own inner world view and also working towards our goals of what we wish to achieve in adulthood. The Anahata Chakra, governed by love, comes into play between the ages of 22-28 when most people find their life partners and consider starting a family. In this time, people also begin to think of ways to contribute positively to the world around them and start philanthropic activities.

Between the ages of 29-35, the Vishuddha Chakra's influence is clearly seen as we find our own voice. We communicate better and gain greater control over our feelings such as anger and fear. This is the time when we are most likely to find a vocation as we seek purpose and meaning in our lives.

The Ajna Chakra, whose main theme is intuition, gains precedence in the ages 36-42 as we are able to look back upon our own life experiences and learn to listen more carefully to our inner guidance mechanism. The ages 43-49 are governed by the Sahasrara Chakra and is often the time when we seek out spirituality, having fulfilled most of our responsibilities towards family and society.

After the age of 50, people were expected to move into the Vanaprastha stage of their life where all their endeavours were to become one with Nature and the Divine, and therefore, the ancient texts do not speak about the role of Chakras beyond this age.

We now come to the heart of the matter – meditation upon the Chakras. The cosmic vibrations contained within the Chakras (which are often the result of cumulative Karmas of several lifetimes) cannot be accessed without two important things – spiritual knowledge and a dedicated practice. So far, the book has covered some of the important aspects of spirituality such as Karma, yoga and Sankhya philosophy and an understanding of the Chakras. It is now time to undertake a practice that will allow you to gradually become aware of the Chakras within your own energy system and in the process, awaken the spiritual energy with dedicated sadhana and commitment to evolve to a higher consciousness.

As with any meditation practice, it is best done every day for 15–20 minutes. Initially, you can start by focusing your attention on one particular Chakra as you familiarise yourself with its energy and vibration. It is ideal to begin with the Muladhara and move upwards rather than to start with say the Anahata Chakra and then randomly move between the higher and lower Chakras. It is important to understand that no Chakra is more important or is of higher status than the other. The idea behind meditating on the Chakras is to gain a better understanding of our own energy fields, and therefore, all Chakras will have to be addressed equally.

Choose a spot where you can sit comfortably with your spine erect. It is fine to rest your back against a chair or cushions. It is important that your posture is one that is comfortable for you as any discomfort will be a major cause of distraction from the meditation. As you focus on a Chakra, look out for any sensations that you may feel such as warmth or a tingling. You may or may not feel any sensations. Both are fine. The important thing is to not judge your meditation experience. Remember to send out an intention to expand and cleanse the Chakra with every breath that you take. Trust your instinct. If you feel that a certain Chakra resonates with a colour that is different from the prescribed one, by all means go with that colour. You can make a chart with the colours and the sounds of each Chakra to serve as a visual guide in your meditation. The use of the Bija Mantra corresponding to each Chakra is highly recommended, but optional. It is best to chant the mantra aloud initially and with practice, internalise it and chant it only mentally after a few weeks/ months.

- Begin the meditation by taking three long, deep breaths and letting go of any pent-up stress or emotions.

- Slowly close your eyes without force and focus on your breath for a few seconds watching the inhale/ exhale.
- When you feel you are sufficiently relaxed, gently bring your attention to the base of your spine at the lowest part of your back which you can sense.
- Visualise a ball of red-coloured light spinning like a disc, getting brighter and brighter with each breath.
- Imagine the dark spots and blemishes disappearing, allowing the red light to become more vivid and warm.
- Chant "Lam".
- Whenever you feel you are ready, move your attention very gently to about two inches below your navel.
- Visualise a bright orange disc of light spinning like a vortex and keep your breath and focus here for as long as is needed.
- Chant "Vam".
- Slowly move your attention to the area just behind your navel.
- Visualise a bright yellow light glowing vividly in the centre of your being. As you focus on this area, allow your mind to send positive intentions of healing and cleansing and feel this yellow colour get more intense and purer.
- Chant "Ram".
- Spend as much time as you need at this Chakra before moving your attention to the region close to your heart and place your hand there for added focus.
- Dwell on the emerald green light that is shining brightly from the centre of the chest and let all impurities, attachments and pain flow out with each exhalation.
- Chant "Yam".
- Move your focus to the area of your throat as you visualise the region awash in a light blue colour, which is refreshing and revitalising the energy in this Chakra.

- Consciously let go of any anger you may be holding on to as you continue to focus on imagining this blue light getting clearer and more vivid with each breath.
- Chant "Hum".
- When you are ready, slowly take your attention to the spot between your eyebrows. You may need to bring your eyeballs together to deepen your focus, but do so at your own comfort.
- Visualise a bright indigo light spinning rapidly between your eyes and feel the energy pulsate as it gathers force, letting go of any blocks or dark spots.
- Chant "Aum".
- Slowly take your attention to the top of your head as you visualise an iridescent white light enveloping your entire being.
- Focus on your breath now as you allow your attention to remain on the white light, and send out intentions of well-being, healing, peace and bliss.
- Keep your attention here for as long as you need and then gently bring your focus back on to your breath. Stay in the calm, relaxed state you have created for yourself for a little while and then slowly get up.

With consistent practice and discipline, you will find that you are able to experience a greater sense of good health and well-being, thus healing physical and emotional wounds which have remained unresolved for too long. You will find that you have a positive outlook on life in general, with an ability to perceive situations more adeptly and handle them with maturity and serenity. The benefits of Chakra meditation are not limited to your physical and mental health alone. This practice will eventually form a basis for your personal transformation and spiritual ascendance.

Namaste

REFERENCES

Text material

From Britannica on topic of Karma

Maya Tiwari: *The Path of Practice: A Woman's Book of Ayurvedic Healing*

David Frawley Yoga & Ayurveda: *Self-Healing and Self-Realization*

Azriel ReShel (Uplift) The Universal Law of Karma

Sadhguru (Isha Foundation)

Olivia Goldhill

Harish Johari: *Chakras: Energy Centres of Transformation*

Marilyn Yalom: *The Amorous Heart: An Unconventional History of Love.*

Deborah Rozman Ph.D.

Judith Anodea: *Wheels of Life*

Judith Anodea: *Eastern Body, Western Mind: Psychology and the Chakra System As a Path to the Self*

Caroline Myss: *Anatomy of the Spirit: The Seven Stages of Power and Healing*

Tiffany Luptak: *The Chakras: Inner Portals to Harmony*

Felise Bermen: *Swadhisthana – the Second Chakra, one's own abode*

Kelly McGonigal: *The Willpower Instinct: How Self-Control Works, Why It Matters, and What You Can Do to Get More of It*

Catarina Lino: *The Psychology of Will Power*

Website URL

adishakti.org/subtle_system/mooladhara_chakra

drvidyahattangadi.com/water-has-memory/

www.psychologytoday.com/us/experts/ilene-strauss-cohen-phd

www.shivashantiyoga.com/the-second-chakra-swadistana-ones-own-abode/

kathycaprino/2018/11/28/three-simple-steps-to-identify-your-life-purpose-and-leverage-it-in-your-career

www.psychologytoday.com/us/blog/think-well/201802/how-respond-criticism

hbr.org/2011/04/strategies-for-learning-from-failure

www.calmwithyoga.com/get-more-mental-clarity-emotional-stability-well-being-by-activating-heart-coherence/

www.swami-krishnananda.org

theophilelancien.org/en/anahata-chakra-3-antelope-sy

daringtolivefully.com/spend-more-time-in-nature

thegoddessgarden.com/throat-chakra-vishuddha-chakra

roamingyogi.co/throat-chakra-vishuddha-chakra-fifth-chakra

www.yogajournal.com/yoga-101/chakratuneup2015-intro-visuddha

www.tantra-kundalini.com/vishuddha/

ancient.eu/shiva

www.adventureyogi.com/blog/chakra-series-vishuddha-chakra/

www.goodnet.org/articles/chakra-healing-how-to-open-your-throat

www.eternalhealthyoga.com/ehy/2018/12/05/vishuddha-chakra-say-say/

yogainternational.com/article/view/4-degrees-of-human-speech

callofthevedas.wordpress.com/2015/10/30/managing-taming-and-dissolving-anger/

tamilandvedas.com/tag/four-types-of-anger/

www.theguardian.com/lifeandstyle/2016/nov/25/how-to-be-a-good-listener-the-experts-guide

hbr.org/2016/07/what-great-listeners-actually-do

www.yogajournal.com/yoga-101/talk-pretty

www.nytimes.com/2017/05/08/smarter-living/why-you-should-learn-to-say-no-more-often

www.yogajournal.com/teach/yoga-and-samkhya-purifying-the-elements-of-the-human-being

www.-anatomy.com/third-eye-chakra.html

www.tantra-kundalini.com/ajna/

www.yogajournal.com/yoga-101/chakratuneup2015-intro-ajna

chopra.com/articles/trust-your-intuition-with-the-sixth-chakra

www.chakras.info/third-eye-chakra/

www.psychologytoday.com/intl/blog/the-intuitive-compass/201108/what-is-intuition-and-how-do-we-use-it

www.huffingtonpost.in/entry/the-habits-of-highly-intuitive-people

www.nei.nih.gov/learn-about-eye-health/healthy-vision/how-eyes-work

www.businessinsider.in/science/a-neuroscientist-explains-why-reality-may-just-be-a-hallucination

yogachicago.com/2014/01/om-the-sacred-pranava-everything-you-wanted-to-know-about-

www.pranava.com/pranava_whatis.html

letitgoyoga.com/indigo-is-the-color-of-the-sixth-chakra

lonerwolf.com/third-eye-chakra-healing/

www.talkspace.com/blog/why-you-should-pay-attention-to-your-dreams/

blogs.psychcentral.com/practical-psychoanalysis/2017/09/5-reasons-to-pay-attention-to-your-dreams

www.ayurvedictalk.com/trataka-a-yoga-form-that-unfolds-the-eyes-mind-relationship yogalondon.net/monkey/users-guide-to-the-chakras-the-sahasrara –

www.chakras.info/crown-chakra/

www.yogiapproved.com/om/the-crown-chakra-how-it-connects-you-to-the-Divine/

lonerwolf.com/crown-chakra-healing/

powerthoughtsmeditationclub.com/the-chakras/

www.yogapedia.com/definition/5370/vairagya

www.esamskriti.com/e/Spirituality/Philosophy/What-is-VAIRAGYA-1.aspx

ausram.blogspot.com/2014/01/an-amazing-verse-from-bhagavad-gita.html

www.speakingtree.in/blog/sadhana-chatushtaya-varanana

www.yogapedia.com/definition/10768/sadhana-chatushtaya

zenhabits.net/simple-living-manifesto-72-ideas-to-simplify-your-life/

medium.com/@zamirdhanji/when-the-student-is-ready-the-master-appears

tayyoga.wordpress.com/2017/12/27/part-16-koshas-and-chakras/

www.amcollege.edu/blog/balancing-chakras

greatergood.berkeley.edu/article/item/how_modern_life_became_disconnected_from_nature

ACKNOWLEDGEMENTS

The lockdown offered me an opportunity to complete the book earlier than expected. Many thanks to the following people without whom the book would not have been possible:

- My daughter Puja who is my sounding board, critic, proof-reader and editor
- My Publishing Manager Hema (Notion Press) for her patience and guidance
- Team Incredible Design (especially Krishan and Sandeep) for the cover design
- Team Bluebrick (especially Velu) for the illustrations and cover page

ALSO BY THIS AUTHOR

Sri Chakra Yantra

Manifest anything with the symbol of everything

Discover how a 12,000-year-old mystical symbol holds the key to awakening your deepest inner potential and enhancing your powers of manifestation.

The Sri Chakra Yantra is an ancient symbol depicting the process of creation in a powerful matrix which represents both the macrocosm (the Universe) and microcosm (the human body), thus acting as a **powerful, cosmic antenna** that allows you direct access to communicate with the Universe.

The book delves into some metaphysical aspects which are reflected in the philosophies underlying Shaktism, Tantra, Dasa Mahavidya and Sri Vidya. Once these concepts throw some light on the basis of Sri Chakra worship, the nature of sacred geometry and the significance, structure and meaning of the Sri Chakra Yantra are explained. This is followed by chapters that focus upon the relationship of the human body to the Sri Chakra and the connection of the Pineal Gland. There is also a brief note on healing and the Sri Chakra.

The use of sounds in the path to spiritual growth is discussed with special focus on the sounds (mantras and stotras) associated with the Sri Chakra Yantra. The book describes the role of mudras and contains details about the initial infusion of energy into the yantra, the method of worship, path to visualisation and meditation on the Sri Chakra.

This book is meant to equip the reader with information and skills necessary to harness the tremendous cosmic energies available in the Universe and channelize it to make life's dreams come true by presenting the Sri Chakra Yantra as a tool for self-development.

THE SRI CHAKRA YANTRA FOUNDATION

The Sri Chakra Yantra Foundation is a not-for-profit organisation created with the intention of bringing individuals and organizations together to improve health and well-being, cultivate spiritual knowledge, expand consciousness and provide authentic information about Tantra and Sri Vidya as outlined in the Hindu Scriptures.

The Foundation conceptualizes, organises and executes activities and initiatives that bring true reformation and change in human minds for a better, more inclusive and truly united world. The key objectives and activities of the Foundation derive from the dual intents of concern for mankind and the search for truth—helping people to explore ways and means to expand their spiritual horizons and lead a multi-dimensional life.

Co-founded by Vinita Rashinkar, author of "Sri Chakra Yantra" and "Chakras", this Foundation is an endeavour to bring together people from across the globe who have an interest in Sri Vidya. Sri Vidya is an ancient Shakta Tantra school of wisdom that is focused on the worship of Shakti, the feminine principle. In the tradition of Sri Vidya, the Self is worshipped as a deity and mantras or sacred sounds are offered to the divinity that lies within us. Sri Vidya is the embodiment of the tantric experience—all forms of tantric practices are subsumed in it.

The four main areas of work that the Foundation is involved in are:

- Education and Research
- Humanitarian causes
- Environment
- Sri Vidya Studies

For more information on the Foundation, please see www.srichakrayantrafoundation.com